Prospects for Research and Development in Education

THE NATIONAL SOCIETY
FOR THE STUDY OF EDUCATION

Series on Contemporary Educational Issues
Kenneth J. Rehage, Series Editor

The 1976 Titles

Prospects for Research and Development in Education, Ralph W.
  Tyler, Editor
Counseling Children and Adolescents, William M. Walsh, Editor
Public Testimony on Public Schools, National Committee for
  Citizens in Education, Commission on Educational Governance

The National Society for the Study of Education also publishes Year-
books which are distributed by the University of Chicago Press. Inquiries regarding all publications of the Society, as well as inquiries
about membership in the Society, may be addressed to the Secretary-
Treasurer, 5835 Kimbark Avenue, Chicago, IL 60637. Membership
in the Society is open to any who are interested in promoting the
investigation and discussion of educational questions.

Prospects for Research and Development in Education

Edited by

RALPH W. TYLER

Director Emeritus
Center for Advanced Study in the
Behavioral Sciences

McCutchan Publishing Corporation
2526 Grove Street
Berkeley, California 94704

ISBN: 0-8211-1906-0
Library of Congress Catalog Card Number: 75-36111

Acknowledgments

John Brademas, "A Congressional View of Educational R & D and NIE," *Educational Researcher*, March 1974, pp. 12-15. Copyright 1974, American Educational Research Association, Washington, D.C.

John B. Carroll, "Basic and Applied Research in Education," *Harvard Educational Review* 38, Spring 1968, pp. 268-273. Copyright © 1968 by President and Fellows of Harvard College.

James J. Gallagher, "The Prospects for Governmental Support of Educational Research," *Educational Researcher*, July-August 1975, pp. 13-14. Copyright 1975, American Educational Research Association, Washington, D.C.

Edith Green, "Federal Funds in Education: When Does Use Become Abuse?" *The Educational Forum*, Volume 36, Number 1 (November 1971), pp. 7-20. Used by permission of Kappa Delta Pi, An Honor Society in Education, P.O. Box A, West Lafayette, Indiana 47906, owners of the copyright.

Egon G. Guba and David L. Clark, "The Configurational Perspective: A New View of Educational Knowledge Production and Utilization," *Educational Researcher*, April 1975, pp. 6-9. Copyright 1975, American Educational Research Association, Washington, D.C.

Sidney P. Marland, Jr., "A New Order of Educational Research and Development," *Phi Delta Kappan* 52 (June 1971), pp. 576-578. Reprinted with permission.

"NIE Plan to Build Educational R & D Capacity," *Educational Researcher*, February 1974, pp. 14-19. Copyright 1974, American Educational Research Association, Washington, D.C.

"On the Record: Support for NIE," *Educational Researcher*, July-August 1975, p. 1. Copyright 1975, American Educational Research Association, Washington, D.C.

Claiborne Pell, "Building Partnerships for Educational Research and Development," *Educational Researcher*, January 1975, pp. 11-12. Copyright 1975, American Educational Research Association, Washington, D.C.

Research for Tomorrow's Schools, ed. Lee J. Cronbach and Patrick Suppes (New York: Macmillan, 1969), pp. 42, 43-48, 49-51, 59-61, 66-68, 89-95, 111-112, 113-117, 171-175, 212-214, 216-218, 249-251. Reprinted with permission of Macmillan Publishing Company, Inc. Copyright © 1969 by The National Academy of Education.

William J. Russell, "AERA's Professional Liaison Program: A New Thrust," *Educational Researcher*, February 1975, pp. 3-4. Copyright 1975, American Educational Research Association, Washington, D.C.

Lindley J. Stiles, "Developing a Research Component for Education," *Journal of Educational Research* 65 (January 1972), pp. 197-202. Reprinted with permission.

Patricia Stivers, "NIE: Learning about Congress the Hard Way," *Educational Researcher*, November 1973, pp. 8-9. Copyright 1973, American Educational Research Association, Washington, D.C.

Patrick Suppes, "The Place of Theory in Educational Research," *Educational Researcher*, June 1974, pp. 4-6, 8-9. Copyright 1974, American Educational Research Association, Washington, D.C.

W. D. Wall, "The Future of Educational Research," *Educational Research* 10 (June 1968), pp. 163-169. With the permission of the National Foundation for Educational Research in England and Wales.

SERIES FOREWORD

Prospects for Research and Development in Education, published under the auspices of the National Society for the Study of Education, is the eighteenth volume to appear in the Society's recently established Series on Contemporary Educational Issues. Like its predecessors, this volume undertakes to inform the profession and the general public about important aspects of a current issue in the field of education. Ralph W. Tyler, the editor, has also assisted in the preparation of two previous publications in the series—*Accountability in Education* (with Leon M. Lessinger) and *Crucial Issues in Testing* (with Richard M. Wolf).

In this volume Dr. Tyler has used his wide-ranging experience and his deep insights most effectively to provide the reader with a broad perspective on the problems of research and development in education. The excerpts from previously published works that he includes, and his comments upon them, give a valuable historical background, highlight current central issues, and set forth some of the alternative futures that can now be envisioned for research and development. A particularly useful contribution of this volume is the effort to make appropriate distinctions between "research" and "development," distinctions that are not always kept clearly in mind.

The Society is greatly indebted to Dr. Tyler for yet another contribution to its publications, as well as to those who have kindly granted permission for us to reprint materials that have been previously published elsewhere.

Kenneth J. Rehage

for the Committee on the Expanded
Publication Program of the
National Society for the Study
of Education

PREFACE

Until the passage of the Cooperative Educational Research Act by the U.S. Congress in 1954, educational research was largely an activity carried on by professors of education during the time not devoted to teaching. The original federal appropriation of less than $1,000,000 gradually increased. With the launching of Sputnik the amount of the appropriation grew rapidly through the funds provided for science education to the National Science Foundation, and the research portions of the National Defense Education Act, in addition to the sharply increased appropriations under the Cooperative Research Program.

The Elementary and Secondary Education Act of 1965 extended the authority of the Office of Education to maintain nonprofit education laboratories as well as university-based research and development centers in education so that by 1969 federal funds in support of educational research and development exceeded $200,000,000. At that time, twenty-one educational laboratories and research and development centers and scores of other centers, institutes, university departments, state departments of education, city school systems, and profit and nonprofit corporations were involved in educational research and development activities. Five years later, half of the federally supported laboratories and research and development centers were either in the process of dissolution or were sharply curtailing their efforts. The National Institute of Education, which had been viewed by many educational researchers as the counterpart in education of the mammoth National Institutes of Health that had transformed, developed, and supported research in the field of health, encountered obstacles in securing appropriations so that federal funds in educational research and development have not increased as anticipated.

What has happened? What are the prospects for educational research and development in the near future? These questions are being raised again and again by practicing educators and interested laymen as well as by researchers and developers. Since the history of educational research is relatively short, there is limited past experience on which to draw in seeking to predict the future. A number of thoughtful leaders in education, politics, and research, however, have expressed their views, have clarified some of the issues, and have exposed some of the misconceptions. Although no consensus is apparent, several alternatives are suggested, and their consequences are outlined.

The purpose of this volume is to help the reader identify the problems, sort out the issues, and formulate some possible alternatives for the future, by assembling, excerpting, and commenting on some of the many articles and other publications dealing with the problems and prospects for educational research and development.

The first chapter deals with the definitions of research and of development and with the confusion often resulting from failure to distinguish the differences between the two. The second chapter furnishes historical perspective, which proves helpful in understanding the current stage of growth and maturation of educational research, particularly in the United States. In the third chapter the political problems involved in obtaining substantial federal support are discussed, while in the fourth allegations concerning the mistakes and shortcomings of recent research and development programs are presented. The fifth chapter outlines several proposals for improving the quality of research, while the sixth deals with the issue of relevance and implementation of development activities. Finally, the seventh chapter briefly summarizes alternative futures for research and development in the field of education.

CONTENTS

1. DEFINITIONS OF RESEARCH AND DEVELOPMENT

There is much confusion over the meaning of the words "research" and "development," particularly when they are applied to social functions, such as education. No standardized definition distinguishes the two words, but one can make a simple distinction in terms of purpose. The purpose of research is to gain greater understanding of a phenomenon, while the purpose of development is to devise and perfect the means to accomplish specified ends under certain conditions. This distinction can be illustrated in the case of Title I programs that are concerned with improving the education of disadvantaged children. Research in connection with these programs is an effort to understand more fully what and how children from homes of poverty learn, including the identification of the difficulties they encounter and the assets they employ in overcoming difficulties in learning. Development is an effort to design educational programs to facilitate their learning. Thus, it is obvious that, as we gain significant knowledge about the children's learning, we have not only a more adequate set of criteria that Title I programs must meet, but we also have added suggestions about features to include in designing programs. In general, the development activities—designing a curriculum, producing instructional devices and materials, devising ways by which teachers and other persons can help students learn, and performing evaluations—involve much greater costs than most research activities.

It usually takes less energy to acquire knowledge than it does to develop and perfect the means by which something can be done with the knowledge.

1

Furthermore, because knowledge is cumulative, one can draw upon a store of existing knowledge gained from experience and research that span centuries of intellectual effort. On the other hand, the actual development requires a contemporary design, the selection or production of materials, the cooperation and education of those who are to employ the new program, a continuing evaluation of its effectiveness, and the making of improvements as needed. Both research and development are important, but their relative costs are different.

It was found in a recent study that few school superintendents in major cities could name any research they had utilized in their decision making, although doubtless they were using some. Project Hindsight, conducted by the Department of Defense to ascertain the source of the knowledge used in developing the modern weapons systems, found that almost all of this knowledge came from research, but that more than 80 percent of the crucial facts and principles came from research that had been conducted at least fifty years earlier. Perhaps the most important products of research are concepts and generalizations about phenomena that soon become part of our normal thinking. We may not realize that this knowledge was originally obtained from research because it has become so widely known, but that is, nevertheless, its source.

As an example, educators today take for granted that children will learn the behavior they practice and find satisfying, but Edward Thorndike's formulation in 1910 of two basic principles of learning, which he called the Law of Exercise and the Law of Effect, was a new conception for many. Thorndike developed these generalizations from an extended series of experiments, first with animals and then with young people. As another example, in 1912 when Charles H. Judd formulated the principle of generalization in learning, a new way of viewing educational objectives was open to educators. Judd's formulation was based on extensive experiments that he and his colleagues conducted first at Yale and then at the University of Chicago. In both of these illustrations, the ideas emerging from the research investigations have become part of the basic knowledge used by educators, most of whom are unable to recall any research results that they utilize in their work.

These illustrations also suggest that research does not consist of simple answers to particular questions. For example, medical research seeks knowledge of such things as how the entire human organism functions, the kinds of effects cancer can have, or the very nature of cancer itself as an abnormal growth process. Research, and science generally, is a social enterprise that involves a whole group of people and resources devoted to seeking understanding of certain phenomena. For example, educational research attempts to understand the psychological operation of the human organism, the way children learn, and the community forces that lead to different kinds of reactions to various educational programs.

Educational research also seeks to provide public verification for its discoveries. Some researchers simply publish their findings; others criticize, verify, and establish this knowledge more systematically. Much of what we think we know has been passed down and accepted without careful checking, and much folklore has been accepted because somebody with prestige or status said it was so. The scientific enterprise that seeks to validate or refute, to verify or deny, to obtain knowledge that is more comprehensive and systematic than commonsense experience is, therefore, essential to man's continuing development. Dependable knowledge is as important for the improvement of education as it is for improvements in all aspects of modern life. However, since education is so pervasive in formal and informal institutions and in all walks of life, and since its functions have been essential throughout man's existence, it is difficult to unravel the many beliefs and practices that may no longer be valid in terms of changing conditions. As we seek higher goals in education, we desperately need more knowledge to guide the endeavor. This need is the primary reason for practitioners to be concerned with the future of educational research.

The Committee on Educational Research of the National Academy of Education has stated the case for systematic educational development. [1]

There is an important distinction between mere developmental activities and developmental (product) research. Design and production can be carried out with no systematic, disciplined inquiry. Indeed, in the course of educational history, most curricula, teaching materials, building designs, etc., have been brought to final form through no more than casual tryout. Until relatively recently this lack of rigor was true of invention and design in all fields of human endeavor. But one field after another—navigation, agriculture, manufacturing, nutrition—has taken the steps forward from folklore to casual empiricism to technology. Controlled measurement and observation have refined products and procedures, with correspondingly better results. Education is only beginning to emerge into a technological phase, and there are many problems in the transition. [2]

Inquiry as an Adjunct to Development

Development, but not educational research, goes on when the university professor attempts to improve his lectures from year to year. His process is simply one of thoughtful self-criticism. A textbook for the national market is prepared on much the same basis. The scale may be different: the draft material tried in a number of classrooms, and opinions solicited from several critics. But the process is still casual and places little burden of proof on the product.

To design educational materials is a creative, imaginative activity, requiring enthusiasm and spontaneity. The most obvious role of disciplined inquiry during development is to be critical: to ask hard and unpopular questions, to find fault, to certify genuine accomplishment while curbing premature enthusiasm. Any critic can play this role, but the research worker brings to bear especially incisive techniques. Perhaps the very incisiveness of research-based criticisms has caused the researcher to be regarded as a hanging judge. But disciplined inquiry, properly used, teams constructively with imagination. It helps the developers to choose between alternative plans that seem equally meritorious. It tests whether an expensive addition to the proposed program is warranted by its results. It clarifies why students have difficulty at certain points and thereby suggests remedies. The observations required for a systematic study may turn up unexpected treasures—for example, the class whose exceptionally good results can be traced to some innovation by its teacher, which can thereafter be made a part of the regular program. But the essential merit of systematic inquiry is that it protects the developer and the school against self-delusion.

The power of facts to cut through unwarranted enthusiasm is illustrated by an incident relatively early in the measurement movement, when tests of character were applied to youths participating in the "character-building" program of a community.[3] This program, which featured recitation of certain moral principles and awards for good behavior, was highly regarded by its leaders and by the community. It was thought to instill ideals of good conduct. The research staff, however, noted how these youths behaved when given opportunities to cheat, not knowing they were observed. It was discovered that boys who had succeeded best in the program—as judged by the number of awards they had won—were *most* likely to cheat. This reversal of expectation led to drastic changes, because the program was evidently encouraging too much interest in reward for its own sake. Without objective research the fault could not have been detected and demonstrated convincingly to the agency directors.

The power that facts on performance have to guide improvement is perhaps most concretely illustrated by the methods used in preparing "programmed" textbooks. These are designed so that the pupil writes one answer after another to questions on successive elements in an explanation. According to the theory by which most programmers operate, if he makes an error the explanation was unclear in some way, or moved too fast. Classroom trials of drafts are essential to make the text effective. Any spot where errors pile up is a spot to be revised in the next draft; often the nature of the errors shows just what is the source of confusion. Similar but less formal microevaluation can be made of any instructional material in draft form.

Product research was significantly lacking from the historical review in an earlier chapter of this book. We saw that developmental *activity* flourished, starting with Dewey's Laboratory School and represented most recently by national curriculum projects in science, mathematics, and other fields. In nearly all these projects, however, data collection has been peripheral and has rarely influenced important decisions. One reason has been the missionary spirit of the usual development project. Only a stoical project director will commission a research staff to be deliberately skeptical. Another reason is that models for product research in education have not been developed, so that no one is very sure what such research can and should attempt to do. (The development of tests is an exception, as we noted in an earlier chapter.)

When research is carried on as part of development—so-called "formative research"[4]—there is not likely to be a public report on it. It is conducted for the private guidance of the developer. Insofar as it makes suggestions, these are incorporated in the product without need to report their origin. Where it notes faults no report is to be expected, as these will be overcome if possible and certainly will not be advertised. Without reports to illustrate what developmental inquiry does, the decision maker does not realize what he can ask of research workers. The investigators themselves lack a realistic picture of the problems and successes of their colleagues in other projects.

The complexity of product research is not well recognized. There is the myth referred to earlier, that development is simply taking a scientific conclusion and putting it into a useful package. There is the myth that describes answering a well-defined question. (This characterizes only research as the conduct of neatly planned experiments, each a small fraction even of conclusion-oriented studies.) There is the myth that one can somehow show that one product "is better" than the next, when results depend on how each is used, and with what students. What is best for one school may not be best everywhere.

Developmental research is untidy. It is disciplined, in that the investigator is expected to be systematic, so that other qualified persons can follow his reasoning. But the process is one of reacting rationally to the unexpected. Though the innovator may be sure what general form his product will take, he will soon find himself deep in problems that call for engineering studies, inventions, or fundamental scientific inquiries.

Sherwin and Isenson,[5] in describing the findings of Project Hindsight, point out that although a new engineering development may double the effectiveness of a piece of military equipment without raising its cost, the improvement cannot be credited to any particular change in design or technology. Rather, the better performance comes from a whole system of changes matched to each other. Even the invention of the transistor could not proceed as a straight application of the semiconductor principle. No less than eight other problems had to be solved with new knowledge or a new engineering concept before efficient devices could be produced.

In addition to the misunderstandings over the distinction between educational research and development, there is some confusion about "basic" and "applied" research in education, particularly research applied to the evaluation of educational programs, practices, devices, and materials of instruction. John Carroll discusses the distinctions between basic and applied research.[6]

. . . it is nevertheless possible to decide, on a fairly objective basis, whether a given scientific task is more immediately addressed to the better understanding of phenomena or to the achievement of a specific practical goal. Any well-designed scientific inquiry contains a series of explicit problems, defined variables, and stated procedures. I would venture the guess that a group of experienced and knowledgeable scientists, upon examination of the design of a scientific investigation, could reach a high degree of agreement on the extent to which it is of a basic or an applied character. It would not be necessary for them to hire a psychologist or a psychiatrist to inquire into the inner motives of the scientist (as Seitz seems to suggest[7]); the motives of the scientist should be manifest in his statement of hypotheses, procedures, and expected results.

Some writers on basic and applied research have attempted to distinguish them with reference to the different reward systems that appear to apply to them. Storer, for example, writes: "Basic research is that which is carried out by a scientist who hopes that his findings will be primarily of interest to his scientific colleagues, while applied research is intended to produce findings which will be of greater interest to the investigator's employer or to the lay public."[8] But Storer's remarks seem simply to point out that there are different ways in which the scientist can, if he chooses, confirm whether his work has the outcomes he himself hopes for it. The basic scientist looks to his scientific colleagues, generally, for affirmation that his work is sound, reasonable, and contributory to the advance of knowledge; the applied scientist gets his signals from his sponsors, who can be expected to reward him in material ways when his discoveries result in useful applications. There will be many scientists, however, for whom these particular reward systems will have little appeal. Fundamentally, the reward system for the scientist or even for a team of scientists is inherent in scientific activity itself. That is, in basic science, effort will be continued until the investigators are rewarded with answers to their questions, while in applied science, efforts will persist until the desired practical ends are achieved.

Public acclaim or disapproval is no criterion either. Both basic and applied scientists will continue their work—as they should, if they are otherwise justified—despite lack of public support. An example of the ridicule that can come from uninformed journalism is to be found in a recent article in the *Reader's Digest*, which holds up to scorn a government-supported research project entitled "Understanding the slump in fourth-grade creativity"[9]—a project that, it happens, was conducted by a well-respected educational researcher (E. P. Torrance) concerning a problem of practical significance to many teachers and parents.

The Dimension of "Relevance"

Much has been said about the evaluation of research in terms of its "relevance" to utilitarian ends. Most frequently, this question is raised about "basic" research: is this research even conceivably relevant to *any* kind of utilitarian end? From the point of view expressed here, this question is thoroughly inappropriate for at least three reasons:

1. The better understanding of phenomena is a legitimate end in itself which can be justified, if necessary, on the ground of the

general experience that at least *some* scientific activity addressed solely to fundamental questions has "paid off" in unexpected practical applications.

2. The potential applications of many basic science researches cannot always immediately be anticipated, even when they do in fact result eventually in practical applications. (The long-delayed application of the discovery of penicillin is a classic case in point.) Often a given scientific finding needs to be further investigated or supplemented before a practical application can be perceived.

3. One can never predict whether a given scientific investigation will be "successful" even in its own terms. We are perhaps unaware of the tremendous amount of scientific activity that is "unsuccessful" in the sense that it fails to yield any new knowledge; further, sometimes a negative result (for example, the failure to confirm a hypothesis or the failure to find a solution to a problem) is a distinct contribution to knowledge because it informs the scientific community that the hypothesis or methodology tried is apparently of no avail. Thus we should not try to evaluate the relevance of a given scientific investigation in terms of its results. Even in the case of "applied science" investigations, the use of this criterion would not be appropriate, for many such studies fail to achieve practical solutions although they are nonetheless clearly so *directed*. To assess relevance, we must concentrate on evaluating the *process* of scientific investigation—the framing of questions and hypotheses, the research design, the analysis of findings, and so on—and not the results.

In this light, basic science investigation is *inherently* relevant (at least to the undefined utilitarian aims mentioned above) when it is addressed to questions that the investigator—if he is well trained and knowledgeable in his field—feels are reasonable and useful to answer, and when in the judgment of his fellow scientists it is properly designed to answer those questions. We shall not insist, however, on the additional qualification that the relevant scientific community also approve the reasonableness of the questions asked because there are a number of cases in the history of science where a lone investigator successfully showed that apparently unreasonable questions were in fact worth pursuing.

We should point out, too, that, except for rare cases, a scientist pursues questions *within a fairly well-defined area*—one for which it is possible to specify in a general way the kinds of practical applications that can be foreseen. We know the kinds of applications that have been made of findings in theoretical physics, in chemistry, in biology, in psychology, or in sociology. We could expect, for example, that work on fundamental processes of learning would have applications, if any, mainly in education—and not, say, in civil engineering; work in molecular biology could be expected to have applications both in learning and in the control of genetics. Relevance is therefore specifiable in general terms, even for the purest of basic research; and it is on this basis that the public can justify the support of basic research even when specific applications are not immediately foreseen. If society cannot find any area of relevance for an *area* of research, the case might be different. But one must be careful even here: in Galileo's time, society rejected large areas of science, and for a long period the Soviet government rejected work in Mendelian genetics. More recently, the practical relevance of learning theory has been debated, even by learning theorists.

Some Further, But Rougher, Distinctions

If basic and applied research can be distinguished in terms of the nature of the work, the kinds of questions investigated, the procedures, and the like, it will be useful to expand on some of these points. No one of them, however, can be used as a sole criterion.

With respect to the questions asked, basic research tends to differ from applied research in the fact that it is more concerned with "understanding" and the attainment of knowledge about fundamental variables and their relationships; the prediction of socially important phenomena is of secondary concern, arising solely out of the laws and relationships discovered; and control of phenomena is often of only incidental interest except to verify a finding. Applied research, however, is generally concerned with the control of socially significant phenomena, or, if control is difficult or impossible, at least their prediction. It is interested in the "understanding" of phenomena in terms of laws and relationships as a basis for prediction and control. Generally it starts with facts and propositions already established in basic science and proceeds to test them in particular situations and/or particular combinations such that extrapolation from basic science is risky.

Correlated with this difference is the fact that basic science, in order to gain a better understanding of the workings of phenomena, is more often concerned with detailed, fundamental processes, such as chemical reaction mechanisms, nerve impulses, or isolated learnings; applied research, on the other hand, is more often concerned with gross, higher-order macroprocesses like wine fermentation, social attitudes, or scholastic achievements, because these are the phenomena one wants to predict or control. In the behavioral sciences, we say that basic research has often to do with a "molecular" level of behavior, while applied research has to do with a "molar" level of behavior. For example, basic research in learning is concerned with the precise combinations of stimulus and response variables that produce certain effects, whereas applied research might be concerned with the effects, say, of massive doses of positive reward, which for certain groups of school learners might *on the average* produce significantly beneficial effects. The applied researcher would not necessarily worry about why positive reward works, or why it does not always work for all students, whereas the basic research scientist—if he is worth his salt—will push for understanding of the total dynamics of the phenomena he is studying. (As soon as the applied researcher starts worrying about deeper questions, he becomes a basic scientist.)

In its concern for processes on a "molecular" level, basic research relies to a greater extent on models of functional relationship that involve relatively small error components, while applied research tends to use models that are more probabilistic and error laden. It is not an accident that statistical procedures were first developed in applied fields of research like certain branches of economics, agriculture, and psychological testing, even though these procedures are, of course, extensively used in basic research even in theoretical physics.

Basic research is more often conducted in the laboratory, or in highly controlled situations, in order to observe the effects of particular variables independently of other possibly relevant variables. Applied research tends to be done in situations that are identical to, or closely similar to, those in which one wants to apply the findings. On the other hand, some basic research is done in relatively uncontrolled situations, and some applied research employs rigorous controls. It is not necessary to suppose that research cannot be basic when it is done in live field situations. In fact, in education there are many arguments for doing certain types of research in such situations. But discussion of this point would take us too far afield.

Basic research is more concerned with the development of theory and of all-embracing models for the explanation of phenomena, while applied research either takes for granted previously established theory and extrapolates from it, or avoids theoretical problems altogether. In any case, basic science stands in a relation of logical priority to applied science. Applied science usually relies heavily upon findings in basic science. It is less often the case that basic science takes off from a finding of applied science; in the instance where this occurs, the purpose usually is to explore the deeper rationale of the finding. Although the essential priority of basic science is not as clear cut in the behavioral and social sciences as it is in the natural sciences, much is to be gained, I think, by following the model of the natural sciences in giving emphasis to basic research at points where applied research cannot make progress alone.

Basic Educational Research

It is thus doubtful, in educational research, that we can move ahead to effective educational engineering without an adequate base in fundamental research in mathematics, computer science, genetics, physiology, psychology, sociology, anthropology, and other relevant disciplines. Particularly where applied research seems to be yielding diminishing dividends, we must turn to basic research on the phenomena in which we are interested. I would propose that such research be called *basic educational research,* and that it be thought of as a part of basic science.

It can be easily demonstrated that many of the most fruitful developments in applied educational technology would have been well-nigh impossible without an adequate foundation in basic research. At the same time, some of these same developments have now reached a point of decreasing returns such that they need a new infusion of results from basic research.

Carroll does not mention specifically educational evaluation and its relation to other kinds of research. It is a generally accepted doctrine today that educational programs and devices and materials of instruction should be evaluated in a continuing and systematic fashion, much as a business enterprise maintains accounting and auditing systems to appraise the continuing performance of its operating programs. Clearly these educational evaluations furnish decision makers useful information regarding the continuing effectiveness or the need for improvement of the programs, devices, and materials. But is this applied research?

All research seeks generalizations that go beyond the specific persons and events studied. Research relating to Title I programs seeks to formulate conceptions and principles applicable to many, if not all, disadvantaged children, or to certain kinds of them. Research on school organization aims to formulate generalizations about different kinds, conditions, and effects of that organization. It is not research if one only learns a great deal about one or several particular disadvantaged children or one or several particular school organizations. Generalizations enable one to understand something about children or organizations that have not been the particular ones under study. Most evaluation studies are appraisals of particular programs, each of which is a complex of curriculum design, the teacher's intentions and activities, instructional devices and materials, and pupils representing a range of interests and abilities, all carried on in a community and school context that has some influence on the way in which the program is implemented. Under these conditions it is difficult to identify meaningful characteristics that are common to a number of programs and thus could serve as a basis for generalizing the evaluation findings. There is much talk about evaluating compensatory education, but most evaluation studies that have made appraisals of particular programs called "compensatory education" have not furnished significant generalizations about it. Hemphill has written on this subject in a chapter in a yearbook of the National Society for the Study of Education. [10] *He says, in part:*

The relationships between research and evaluation studies need to be made explicit. It is evident that many of the activities associated with evaluation in education are also associated with educational research. In many instances, no distinctions are made between evaluation and research. Are evaluation studies to be considered simply a subset of the more general set of activities denoted by the term "research," or are there characteristics of the activities involved in evaluation that can or should be used to distinguish it from research?

Let us first look at the broad objectives of research and of evaluation as they can now be observed in the field of education. It appears to be well agreed that the objective of educational research is to add to our knowledge of the practices and methods of education. Less agreement is evident, however, as to whether new knowledge created by educational research should have some immediate usefulness or whether such research is sufficiently justified by the potential value of any new knowledge or by the satisfaction of any "idle curiosity."[11] Distinctions between "applied research" and "basic research" are often based on considerations of immediate utility as opposed to a concern for the possible usefulness of specific new knowledge. Evaluation studies are made to provide a basis for making decisions about alternatives, and, therefore, in undertaking an evaluation study, one at once addresses himself to questions of utility. It may be objected, however, that this is too idealistic a view of the purpose of evaluation studies. In fact, it may be that the great majority of evaluation studies in education are not concerned with the alternatives per se, but instead deal with the simple question, "Does treatment X work?" At best, there may be an implicit assumption that if X does not work, something else must be tried; but this is as far as thinking about alternatives may go. Regardless of the lack of precision in thinking, providing information for choice among alternatives remains the basic and utilitarian purpose of evaluation studies. It appears that in this respect, at least, it is necessary to regard research, particularly basic research, as having a distinctly different objective than evaluation. Often the information to be provided by an evaluation study is needed because a decision *must* be made. This decision making is not usually an integral part of the evaluation study itself, but a subsequent activity and one to be engaged in by parties not involved in the study. This fact might lead to the conclusion that an evaluation study could avoid questions of value and utility, leaving them to the decision maker, and thus not need to be distinguished from research, either basic or applied. The crux of the issue, however, is not *who* makes a decision about what alternatives or *what information* serves as the basis for a decision; rather, it is *the degree to which concern with value questions is part and parcel of the study.* Decision makers can and frequently do make use of information developed through research, but this act does not thereby transform a research study into an evaluation study.

Evaluation studies differ from research in the manner in which value questions are involved—especially value questions that undergird choices about what information or knowledge is sought. The implications of primacy of utility in evaluation studies and the relative unimportance of such considerations in research are profound. Although there are differences in points of view among behavioral scientists, an "ideal" research study is one in which:

1. Problem selection and definition are the responsibility of the individual doing the research.

2. Tentative answers (hypotheses) to the problem may be derived by deduction from theories or by induction from an organized body of knowledge.

3. Value judgments by the researcher are limited to those implicit in the selection of the problem.

4. Given the statement of the problem and the hypothesis, the research can be replicated.

5. The data to be collected are determined largely by the problem and the hypothesis.

6. Relevant variables can be controlled or manipulated, and systematic effects of other variables can be eliminated by randomization.

The evaluation study may be described in terms of characteristics almost the reverse of those outlined above:

1. The problem is almost completely determined by the situation in which the study is conducted. Many people may be involved in its definition, and, because of its complexity, the problem initially is difficult to define.

2. Precise hypotheses usually cannot be generated; rather the task becomes one of testing generalizations from a variety of research studies, some of which are basically contradictory. There are many gaps which in the absence of verified knowledge must be filled by reliance on judgment and experience.

3. Value judgments are made explicit in the selection and the definition of the problem as well as in the development and implementation of the procedures of the study.

4. The study is unique to a situation and seldom can be replicated, even approximately.

5. The data to be collected are heavily influenced if not determined by feasibility. Choices, when possible, reflect value judgments of decision makers or of those who set policy. There are often large differences between data for which the collection is feasible and data which are of most value to the decision makers.

6. Only superficial control of a multitude of variables important to interpretation of results is possible. Randomization to eliminate the systematic effects of these variables is extremely difficult or impractical to accomplish.[12]

Evaluation studies are often undertaken in response to a need to know the usefulness of an invented alternative to an existing mode of action which has resulted from some combination of old and new knowledge, or they may be undertaken to determine how well an existing mode of action is working. Is a new method of training teachers an improvement over a presently used method? Is a specific head-start program effective in preparing disadvantaged youngsters to enter school? New alternatives are likely to have been based, at least in part, upon generalizations from research findings and results. To the degree that this is true, an evaluation study can provide a test of the generalization and thus go beyond the point at which most research stops—the verification of hypotheses within only a very controlled and restricted situation. In this respect, evaluation can contribute side by side, but in a distinctly important way, to the development of a science of education.

Several reasons led to the inclusion of a chapter in this volume dealing with the distinctions between research and development, between basic and applied research, and between research and evaluation. All of them are commonly included in the broad term "educational research and development." But they have different functions in the total field of education, they are commonly carried on by different people, their costs are in different orders of magnitude, and their support, in the past at least, has come from different sources. These differences should be taken into account in considering the prospects for educational research and development in the future.

Notes

1. *Research for Tomorrow's Schools,* ed. Lee Cronbach and Patrick Suppes (New York: Macmillan, 1969), 171-175.

2. Anthony C. Oettinger, "The Myths of Educational Technology," *Saturday Review* 51 (May 18, 1969): 76, 77 ff.

3. J. B. Maller, "Personality Tests," in *Personality and the Behavior Disorders,* Vol. I, ed. Joseph McV. Hunt (New York: Ronald Press, 1944), 170-213.

4. Michael Scriven, "The Methodology of Evaluation," in *Perspectives of Curriculum Evaluation,* ed. Ralph W. Tyler *et al.* (Chicago: Rand McNally, 1967), 39-83.

5. Chalmers Sherwin and R. S. Isenson, "Project Hindsight," *Science* 156 (June 1967): 1571-1577.

6. John B. Carroll, "Basic and Applied Research in Education," *Harvard Educational Review* 38 (Spring 1968): 268-275.

7. Frederick Seitz, in *Government and Science,* Hearings before the

Subcommittee on Science, Research, and Development of the House Committee on Science and Astronautics, 88th Congress, 1st Session (Washington, D. C.: U.S. Government Printing Office, 1963), 283.

8. N. W. Storer, *Basic versus Applied Research: The Conflict between Means and Ends in Science* (Cambridge, Mass.: Harvard University Press, 1964).

9. A. W. Schulz, "The Great Research Boondoggle," *Reader's Digest* 90 (March 1967): 91-96.

10. John K. Hemphill, "The Relation between Research and Evaluation Studies," in *Educational Evaluation: New Roles, New Means,* ed. Ralph W. Tyler, Sixty-eighth Yearbook of the National Society for the Study of Education, Part II (Chicago: University of Chicago Press, 1969), 189-192.

11. Thorstein Veblen, *The Place of Science in Modern Civilization and Other Essays* (New York: Viking Press, 1919).

12. I am indebted to Dr. Richard Watkins for the major portion of this analysis.

2. HISTORICAL PERSPECTIVE

Although educational research has a short history, some sense of its growth and direction can be obtained from a report of the Committee on Educational Research of the National Academy of Education. The following excerpt from a summary paragraph of that report provides a brief historical perspective with regard to the period 1855-1895:[1]

In the first period of educational leadership in America, the style was collection, collation, and dissemination of facts. Just as the curriculum of the time contained a large element of knowledge for its own sake, so [Henry] Barnard and [William T.] Harris and General [John] Eaton [all U.S. commissioners of education] . . . seemed satisfied that diffusion of information would in itself produce sounder management of schools. Similarly, the curriculum reformers were engaged primarily in the popularization of ideas that seemed to come largely from European sources. American educators, of course, debated the various proposals for changes in the schools, but systematic analysis and testing of proposals came to the fore only at the very end of the period. What native theorizing there was seemed not to go beyond speculation, of the genre of Harris's Hegelianism.

The committee labels the period 1895-1938 "The Heyday of Empiricism."
Some of their comments on that era follow:[2]

The 1890s brought a sweeping change in the intellectual orientation of American society. An unprecedented consciousness of national
power, an emerging urban industrial society, and the sudden adoption
of science as the source of truth set the stage for a questioning of
tradition in every form. It was an age of quickening interest in the
scientific exploration of social and natural phenomena and of high
hope concerning the social benefits of such exploration. It was an age
of scientific enthusiasm not only among scholars, but also among the
lay audiences that devoured the popularized science of such maga-
zines as *The Forum, Popular Science Monthly, The Saturday Evening
Post,* and *The World's Work;* it was an age of heady optimism based
on the widely held belief that science had won the day, and now had
only to transform the world. Not surprisingly it was also an age when
education became a matter for scientific investigation, controlled
experiment, and rational reform: Thorndike and other psychologists
drew practical recommendations from studies of learning; Franklin
Bobbitt and other curriculum makers revised courses of study on
the basis of systematic observations of contemporary society; and
George Strayer and other administrators formulated policy recommendations founded on quantitative analyses of school performance.
And all made common cause with a generation of practical-minded
schoolmen seeking answers to Herbert Spencer's insistent question,
"What knowledge is of most worth?"

This period is of special significance for this report because it
demonstrates much of what research can accomplish at the same time
that it reveals how institutions and philosophies can circumscribe
those achievements. A number of the significant contributions of the
period can be mentioned briefly, with fuller details on some to be
given later. Perhaps most important was the widespread acceptance
of pupil accomplishment as the fundamental test of the educational
program. This change, replacing argumentation from a priori principles
with an appeal to evidence, made it possible to banish misconceptions
and to narrow the ground of controversy. Many an ancient claim was
exploded—most notably, the belief that the pupil who grinds away
at an academically difficult subject is sure to develop his intellectual
powers. A substantial beginning was made toward a psychological

analysis of each school subject. A technology for the measurement of aptitude was developed. And penetrating inquiries were made regarding the nature and development of mental health and character.

Gains were not confined to the psychological aspects of education. Decisions about curriculum that had formerly been settled by pronouncements from committees came more and more to rest on careful assessment of the manpower needs of society and of the tasks persons in various roles actually perform. Matters long taken for granted were freshly examined; certain grammatical expressions roundly condemned in the schoolbooks were found to be commonplace and accepted in the actual speech and writing of cultivated persons, and hence "usage" supplemented grammar as the basis of courses in English. And certain demonstrated facts led to new reflections on educational policy—for example, the finding that the income of an adolescent's family had more to do with his attending college than his ability, and the related finding that he was far more likely to attend a college if one were located near his home.

The journalistic exposés of Joseph Mayer Rice pictured the machine that was the American school in the 1890s: syllabuses and textbooks prescribed the course of study; the responsibility of the pupil was to master the material that would appear on examinations; the responsibility of the teacher was to assist the pupil to that mastery, relying principally on incessant drill and unreflecting discipline.[3] Four decades later the 1938 Yearbook of the National Society for the Study of Education could point to an almost wholly new curriculum, with an elective system that spanned dozens of school subjects; to a range of instructional methods that embraced laboratories, field trips, visual aids, and school libraries; to consolidated high schools offering vocational as well as academic curricula; to vocational guidance programs and diagnostic services directed by school psychologists; to school buildings designed for educational efficiency and built to high standards; and to enormous advances in the preparation, style of work, and salaries of teachers.

Educational improvement in the later nineteenth century had come largely from the requirements of the American democratic experiment, though it had been leavened by pedagogical ideas of European philosophers. Better schooling in the earlier twentieth century grew out of the transformations wrought by industrialism, but it was profoundly influenced by the characteristically American psychology of William James and his pupils G. Stanley Hall and Edward Thorndike.

James and Hall, prominent equally in the academic world and as writers and speakers to the general public, stand at the dividing point between the first and second periods. James rejected the quantitative experimental techniques of the German laboratories, but he saw enough promise in an observational approach to the study of the mind to have founded his own experimental laboratory four years before Wundt's in Leipzig. Through his freshly written textbooks and lectures—many of them directed to teachers—James brought the problems of integrative, adaptive behavior to the fore, while the German psychologists and their more orthodox American disciples were doggedly tabulating isolated sensations. For all his ability to reason and his readiness to seek evidence, James's common sense was the most prominent element in his writings. An example is this well-known passage from his *Talks to Teachers* that has profound relevance for this report.

... you make a great, a very great mistake, if you think that psychology, being the science of the mind's laws, is something from which you can deduce definite programmes and schemes and methods of instruction for immediate schoolroom use. Psychology is a science, and teaching is an art; and sciences never generate arts directly out of themselves. An intermediary inventive mind must make the application, by using its originality . . . .

Everywhere teaching must *agree* with the psychology, but need not necessarily be the only kind of teaching that would so agree.[4]

Hall's interest were even broader than James's, though his curiosity and enthusiasm often seemed to outrun his self-critical discipline as a researcher. But Hall did gather data, and indeed was a pioneer in the fruitful application of the questionnaire method. His most lasting influence on American education was his inauguration of the child-study movement, which provided popular and scholarly support for efforts to liberalize the curriculum.

The turn of the century also witnessed the arrival on the educational scene of John Dewey, Thorstein Veblen, Paul Monroe, E. L. Thorndike, and Joseph Mayer Rice, to be followed soon after by Charles H. Judd, Lewis Terman, George Strayer, Ellwood P. Cubberley, and Franklin Bobbitt. From these men came trenchant social criticisms, new devices for data collection and analysis, and energetic surveys of school practice. They presided over the emergence of graduate study in education, notably at Teachers College of Columbia University, at the University of Chicago, and at Stanford University. They set the patterns for the state, city, and university research bureaus that sprang up across the country, and for the laboratory schools that grew up on the model of the Dewey venture at Chicago.

Joseph Mayer Rice, the liberal muckraking pediatrician who made a career of school reform, is often credited as the founder of empirical scholarship in education. Inspired by the teaching he observed in Germany, he found himself appalled by the mechanical, nonreflective, noncreative character of American schools and set out to bring them into line with the new emphasis on interesting, reflective classroom activity that he had encountered abroad. Singling out the blight of endless rote spelling drills, he thought it would be a simple matter to collect facts to show that these could be reduced without loss, and thus persuade the authorities to release time to more intellectual activities. A large number of schools administered spelling tests of Rice's devising to some 16,000 students in the years 1895-1897, in a crude forerunner of today's National Assessment of Educational Progress. As Rice anticipated, the pupils' attainment on his tests bore no relation to the number of minutes per week their schools devoted to spelling. "The presentation of the results," Leonard Ayres wrote years later, "brought upon the investigator almost unlimited attack. The educators . . . united in denouncing as foolish, reprehensible, and from every point of view indefensible, the effort to discover anything about the value of the teaching of spelling by finding out whether or not the children could spell."[5] Rice, though a member of the National Education Association, was an "outsider" criticizing the profession, and there was no place of honor for such a man . . . .

Although Rice found educators unready to acknowledge hard facts, the situation soon changed. The larger community was coming to be dominated by business ideals in which a favorable balance sheet was the only acceptable evidence of successful management. As Raymond Callahan has documented, the educators were soon parodying the excesses of stopwatch management in industry, talking solemnly about return on investment per pupil and about the number of recitations in Greek that could be purchased for a dollar.[6] The absurdity quickly infected instructional practice; if superintendents were to be judged by the number of pupils turned out per dollar, teachers were to be judged by the number of pupils they could pass on to the next grade. It soon became the practice to pass nearly every student each June, regardless of the quality of his schoolwork.

But quality was not always ignored. Rice had demonstrated that applying an objective test uniformly in many schools is sure to stir up educational debates, and soon there were scales for appraising achievement in handwriting, arithmetic, spelling, drawing, reading, and, eventually, every other school subject. At the same time, intelligence testing was being developed. By 1918, Walter S. Monroe [7] could describe over a hundred well-regarded standardized tests of pupil performance. The tests served the iconoclasm of the new educational scholarship well. Thorndike's famous study, in which he concluded that the study of bookkeeping does just as much to develop testable mental ability as the study of Greek, was dynamite in the hands of the utilitarians who condemned the traditional academic education for doing nothing to prepare high school graduates for "useful work."

The committee describes the laboratory schools that were established during this period:[8]

A major event in the launching of the new era of inquiry was the establishment in 1896 of John Dewey's Laboratory School at the University of Chicago. "Practice schools" had been in operation since the first teacher-training institutions appeared before the Civil War; and "model schools" had grown up in the 1880s and 1890s in connection with the Cook County Normal School and Columbia's Teachers College. But while such schools may well have been models of innovation and excellence, they were not seriously concerned with inquiry. What was new about the Laboratory School was the explicit intention of using it to test hypotheses in practice.

Dewey had been a firm advocate of psychological research as a means of understanding education, but he had no hope that psychological studies alone would show what schools should do. As he said in an 1897 reply to critics of the child-study movement:

Many of the criticisms proceed from a failure to draw the lines carefully between those aspects of child study which belong to the province of the scientific investigator and those which interest the educator. It takes time to develop scientific method, to collect and sift facts, and to derive theoretic conclusions.

There is no more sense in attacking the scientific investigator in this line because he doesn't provide on demand usable recipes, ticketed and labeled for all pedagogical emergencies, than there would have been in attacking the early pioneers in electricity because they worked quietly in the laboratory upon seemingly remote and abstruse subjects instead of providing us offhand with the telegraph, telephone, electric light, and transportation.[9]

Dewey's school was an attempt to work out practical techniques; he was concerned with development and demonstration. For all the school's claim to be a laboratory, the papers emanating from its staff strongly suggest that the inspiring of emulation took precedence over inquiry. Many of the premises of the school's program were articles of faith from the outset. Thus, writing in the *University Record* in 1896, Dewey announced an intention to test the hypothesis that the school is a social institution. He touched on four more specific problems: how to bring the school into closer relation with the home and neighborhood; how to introduce history, science, and art so that they have significance in the light of the child's experience; how to obtain progress in reading, writing, and arithmetic as a by-product of other subjects and activities; and how best to demonstrate the benefits of individual attention secured by small groupings of children and large numbers of teachers.[10] In reading the voluminous literature of the school between 1896 and 1904, one is struck constantly by the problem of how to know when a hypothesis had been established. The continuing attempt to rationalize content and method was surely a contribution to education. Yet for all Dewey's pragmatism it is not clear that he was seeking objective evidence of the strengths and weaknesses of the new proposals.

The fact that this first well-led Laboratory School did not carry on disciplined inquiry and did not produce well-substantiated results is noteworthy because it presages the promotional emphasis and neglect of hypothesis testing that marked later laboratory schools. But it would be captious to criticize Dewey personally for what he did in those eight years. At that time the methods for testing educational hypotheses were little developed, and even James relied as much on anecdote as on research for his conclusions. Dewey founded the school as an act of faith, and his failure to develop a science of classroom experimentation is very likely attributable to the success of his proposals. His ideas had wide appeal, and he was therefore deprived of the stubborn and articulate opposition that may push a man to collect solid evidence. Thorndike was more fortunate. His arguments regarding transfer opposed the interests of teachers of the classics and other subjects, and he was therefore pressed to elaborate his views and to amass evidence for them. If Dewey had been so pressed, he might have been more explicit on such matters as the significance of making learning purposeful rather than merely interesting, and the importance of subject-matter knowledge even in a progressive curriculum. Had he spelled out these concepts, the progressive movement might have been saved from ultimate self-caricature and collapse.

The laboratory schools were limited in their impact because many educators believed that they were too distinctive to serve as models for the majority of the nation's schools. Their advantages in the form of well-equipped facilities, superior teachers, and selected pupils were so apparent that what they demonstrated seemed irrelevant to ordinary institutions. Dewey spoke clearly on this matter in the early days of the Chicago venture:

> As it is not the primary function of a laboratory to devise ways and means that can at once be put to practical use, so it is not the primary purpose of the school to devise methods with reference to their direct application in the graded school system . . . . It is the function of some schools to create new standards and ideals and thus to lead to a gradual change in conditions.[11]

> There is a difference between working out and testing a new truth, or a new method, and applying it on a wide scale, making it available for the mass of men, making it commercial. But the first thing is to discover the truth, to afford all necessary facilities, for this is the most practical thing in the world in the long run. We do not expect to have other schools literally imitate what we do. A working model is not something to be copied; it is to afford a demonstration of the feasibility of the principle, and of the methods which make it feasible.[12]

The separation of education from the arts and sciences during this period had serious effects upon educational research, as the committee has noted:[13]

One manifestation of the emergence of education as a self-consciously independent profession was the sharp separation of education from the arts and sciences that gradually developed in the years following 1905.[14] Before that time, a fairly warm spirit of cooperation had marked the relations between academic scholars and professional educators. If one takes the NEA as an example, men such as President Eliot of Harvard and President Gilman of Johns

Hopkins worked closely with well-known superintendents of schools such as William B. Maxwell and with leading professors of education such as Charles DeGarmo and Charles and Frank McMurray. That Butler could feel as he did about Harris, the most noted professional educator of his day, is indicative of the respectful cooperation.

The rift between the more pragmatically oriented educators and the more traditionally oriented academicians is dramatically conveyed by the same Butler who had waxed eloquent over his "vigorous and enthusiastic service" to the National Education Association from 1885 to 1905. After that date he complained that the organization, once a body of genuine educational leaders who were dealing with ideas and institutions, had degenerated into a large popular assembly dominated by a very inferior class of teachers and school officials whose main object appeared to be personal advancement.[15] However much personal conflicts may have led Butler to this harsh allegation, it was patently a reflection of two larger social phenomena: the popularization of schooling and the professionalization of teaching.

The universities responded to the demand for more and better education by establishing independent faculties of education. Whatever they gained in the short run by way of vigorous attention to education must be weighed against the attenuation of the critical and independent influence of the disciplines. Pressed to advise the schoolman, the scholar in the education faculty found himself encouraged to pontificate and to draw concrete, unrestricted conclusions about proper practice from investigations either too limited to produce dependable results or too broad to sustain a disciplined attack.

For various reasons, academic specialists in the arts and sciences turned their attention away from the educational aspects of their fields so that by 1940 the separation was nearly complete. There were exceptions, to be sure: Charles Merriam and Charles Beard in political science, William Waller and the Lynds in sociology, Merle Curti and Samuel Eliot Morison in history. But the professions of educational sociology, educational psychology, educational philosophy, and educational history became separated from the main body of their disciplines. Few scholars outside schools of education read and commented on works related to education. Dewey, for example, once stated that his best presentation of his general philosophy was *Democracy and Education,* but he complained that philosophers had remained unfamiliar with the book because of its title.

Educational research and the training of educational researchers became a specialty of professors of education. Between 1897 and 1920s, the leading professors of education were recruited directly from the disciplines and remained leading figures in their academic fields. In the 1920s the influential chairs began to fall to the students trained by the first generation of education professors. An educational sociologist, say, who had studied under one professional sociologist, and under a dozen professors of education having other intellectual commitments, could not be deeply grounded in sociology. Moreover, he was likely to have been indoctrinated with some particular view of what "the new education" ought to be.

Equally enfeebling was a glorification of breadth that often made it respectable for a single professor of education to serve as expert over the whole range of history, philosophy, sociology, and perhaps psychology as well. (The argument for integrative thinking may have been no more than a rationalization of the fact that the education faculty of that time could not afford to hire men to cultivate each area.) Meanwhile, students recruited into education courses were often more motivated toward benefiting people here and now than toward the pursuit of knowledge. Hence, the profession came to contain fewer men who challenged the current assumptions, and fewer "breakthroughs" occurred. If the quality of the best research did not decline, it failed to advance beyond the early models in the field.

As a result, the training of researchers declined seriously in quality. By 1941, T. R. McConnell[16] found himself obliged to restate a number of elementary propositions that should have been obvious to his colleagues in education. Thorough knowledge of the relevant phases of the basic discipline, he insisted, is a prerequisite for any sound educational research: studies of school finance must rest on a sound understanding of all public finance; studies of educational growth must be based on an understanding of child development in general. But by the 1940s, a few educational researchers were qualified along such lines, and most universities were granting research degrees to students in education who had not taken a single graduate course in a field of the arts and sciences.

In concluding its historical essay on American scholars and educational progress, the committee characterizes the period 1938-1958 as one in which "Promotional Activity Supplements Inquiry."[17]

After the 1920s there was a gradual shift toward using research as an agent of change. The famous Eight-Year Study of the Progressive Education Association is a superior example. The study was initiated to determine whether subject-matter requirements for college entrance, which seemed to limit efforts to modernize high school curricula, were justified. The investigators suggested that such requirements be abolished for graduates of a selected group of schools, proposing that for experimental purposes any recommended graduate of those schools be admitted to college no matter what subjects he had studied. They proposed to compare the success of these students with that of students who had fulfilled conventional requirements in equally good high schools. This study was an unprecedented co-operative effort between thirty high school faculties and a large, well-led central "evaluation staff."

Although the study was carried out as planned, one cannot escape the impression that the central question was of minor interest to the investigators and the educational community. The main contribution of the study was to encourage the experimental schools to explore new teaching and counseling procedures. A subunit of the research staff did carry out the systematic follow-up study and did report that the experimental students "were significantly superior" in college performance.[18] When the report appeared, critics[19] argued that one could only claim that the experimental procedures had done no harm to the student's future academic career; the design of the study, they said, was biased in favor of the experimental schools. The fact that little attention was given to this criticism itself shows that few persons cared at this time about a scientific foundation for educational policy.

The main enterprise of the evaluation staff was to assist teachers in examining their own work. The staff developed ingenious procedures for studying educational outcomes other than factual knowledge and skill, procedures that have left a lasting mark on educational research and educational objectives. The staff members worked with teachers of each subject in each school on an individual basis; yet in the end there was a rather remarkable concurrence between the "local objectives" arrived at in the schools and the measuring instruments the staff brought with them from Chicago. The data on student performance were used primarily by the teachers involved, rather than by administrators and school boards, and there was virtually no attempt to draw publishable conclusions from the data. As in Dewey's Laboratory School, there was an initial faith that the experimental schools were proceeding along the right line, and no urge to challenge the innovations.

The social reformers and the progressive educators were essentially crusaders, not open-minded inquirers. Facts were occasionally gathered to demonstrate the need for a social change that had already been judged desirable in advance, or to monitor an operation so as to modify its details. Insofar as the crusade continued into the late 1940s and 1950s, its research stayed safely away from the aims and content of education; on that, minds were made up, and dissent was ignored. The topics left open for research were the personal relationships among teachers, among pupils, and between teachers and pupils, the psychology and sociology of individual differences, and the nature and character of the counseling process.

A teacher-training activity known as "action research" absorbed at least as much professorial effort as more conventional inquiry, and attracted far more attention in the schools. Guided by the Eight-Year Study and the pattern used by the late Kurt Lewin to alter housewives' food-buying habits during World War II, persons seeking to change instruction set up projects in local schools under the leadership of visiting university professors. The cooperating teachers would identify some suspected inadequacy in their local program, collect facts by means of fairly unsophisticated instruments, plan some change on the basis of the facts, carry it out, and collect follow-up data. The goal was to change the practices of the teachers. The leaders of "action research" were convinced that nothing could be gained from conclusion-oriented research, that a study done in one school could not, through communication of findings, influence what was being done in the next.[20] Because the studies were usually for local use, they were not subjected to the cross fire of discussion and competent criticism that is an essential part of disciplined inquiry, and they cannot be judged as research. No doubt in some settings and under particular leaders the studies were truly self-critical, decision-oriented inquiries that directly improved the local program;

no doubt in other instances the entire activity was a disguised method of manipulating teachers to move in certain approved directions.

The report of the Committee on Educational Research of the National Academy of Education also presented a few extended examples of the interplay among inquiry, theory, and practice to illustrate operations of educational research in our immediate past. Less well known to most of us are the examples of philosophic research and historical inquiry. The work of Charles Peirce is used as the illustration of philosophy.[21]

Aside from his decisive influence on James and Dewey, and on the philosophy of pragmatism generally, Peirce is of interest because of his pioneering work in bringing scientific conceptions and attitudes to bear on philosophy, and in making explicit and defending "the laboratory habit of mind." His contributions to symbolic logic, to the theory of probability, induction, and measurement, to the philosophy of logic and symbolism, to the theory of definition and the analysis of belief—all are motivated by an overriding concern with clarifying the relevance and implications of scientific logic for critical thought and action. In terms of his notion of scientific logic, Peirce criticized not only classical rationalistic philosophy, but also nineteenth-century romanticism and positivism, proposing *logical method* as a unifying conception applicable not only to science but to life. For Peirce the essence of a general education was to be found in this conception of a general logical method that emphasizes the clarity of concepts and critical reasoning, the method being exemplified in modern scientific practice. In elaborating his conception, he developed an explicit formulation of what are now widely recognized as elements of scientific thought: a rejection of the idea that findings can ever be certain and final, an emphasis on probability and hypothetical reasoning, a conception of operational definition, a public notion of science as a community of investigators, a problem approach to inquiry, and a view of axioms as tentative assumptions to be tested in experience.

Translated into educational terms, many of these emphases are recognizable and familiar in pragmatic notions of schooling: the attempt to link thought and action, the effort to structure teaching around problems, the rejection of the quest for certainty and the corresponding effort to develop probabilistic modes of reasoning, the emphasis on publicly available evidence, and the primary stress on methods of arriving at knowledge rather than on the knowledge already stored up. Note that Peirce's motivations were primarily theoretical and philosophical; he himself did not translate his key notions into educational applications. Nevertheless, his general concern with modernizing our logical conceptions turned out to have significant, if indirect, effects on educational thinking and practice.

Knowledge as the Fruit of Problem Solving

We cannot undertake to review the various facets of Peirce's philosophy; but, to indicate the nature of his work, we shall sketch some of his general lines of argument against the rationalistic view of knowledge exemplified, in particular, by Descartes. Descartes (1596-1650)—who, in freeing himself from authoritarianism, founded modern philosophy—had counseled adoption of a method of radical doubt. His aim was to achieve certainty, and his method was deductive. Construing knowledge after the model of a mathematical system, he wanted to start with clear, distinct, and hence indubitable premises accessible to introspection, and then to move with deductive certainty step by step to an indubitable conclusion. His conception of science was that of a chain of linear reasoning resting upon a foundation invulnerable to doubt, the whole chain as strong as its weakest link. Descartes's starting point was his own indubitable existence, given immediately in the fact of his own conscious thinking: "Cogito ergo sum."

In his paper "Some Consequences of Four Incapacities" Peirce argues that "modern science and modern logic require us to stand upon a very different platform from this."[22] Radical doubt is an impossible method, he argues, for inquiry can never wipe the slate clean in order to start with foundations that are truly certain. "We must begin with all the prejudices which we actually have when we enter upon the study of philosophy . . . . Let us not pretend to doubt in philosophy what we do not doubt in our hearts." We begin always in the middle of things, taking for granted a whole mass of assumptions while we test the particular one that is thrown into doubt.

Doubt, he urges, cannot be produced at will by following a philosophical maxim. It is an active state of irritation, not the mere absence of belief. In inquiry, thought struggles to pass from real doubt to belief, a latent state of readiness or habit that sets us to act in selective ways in the future. Inquiry never starts afresh, but operates with assumptions while it focuses upon genuine issues in doubt, defining a problem. The researcher takes for granted a variety of theories, laws, and factual assumptions in the process of testing some view that is the core of the issue presently in doubt. Afterward, should one of his prior assumptions be itself put in doubt, he may appropriately set himself to testing that one. But he cannot throw all his beliefs into doubt simultaneously, and to claim to do so is self-deception.

Nor, argues Peirce, can certainty be found in the individual consciousness. "Metaphysicians will all agree that metaphysics has reached a pitch of certainty far beyond that of the physical sciences—only they can agree upon nothing else," he writes. If one contrasts the sciences, in which men do come to agreement, theories are in a state of suspension until agreement is reached, whereupon—though the theory is known not to be a final one—the issue of certainty becomes idle. The relevant criterion is then not the subjective conviction of the individual consciousness, but the agreement of disciplined minds in the community of scientific investigators, an ineradicably public criterion which is built into scientific modes of thought. There is, in fact, no possibility that certainty will be found through introspection, for all thinking is inherently symbolic and general as well as hypothetical, "all knowledge of the internal world" being derived "by hypothetical reasoning from our knowledge of external facts."

Finally, the Cartesian conception of linear deductive reasoning from indubitable foundations is to be rejected in favor of the weaving together of a circumstantial fabric from many different strands. "Philosophy," writes Peirce, "ought to imitate the successful sciences in its methods, so far as to proceed only from tangible premises which can be subjected to careful scrutiny, and to trust rather to the multitude and variety of its arguments than to the conclusiveness of any one. Its reasoning should not form a chain which is no stronger than its weakest link, but a cable whose fibers may be ever so slender, provided they are sufficiently numerous and intimately connected."

The whole Cartesian conception of knowledge is thus rejected. The ideal of certainty is replaced by that of fallible hypothetical assumptions, the notion of radical doubt replaced by the selective doubt that focuses upon a well-defined problem, the conception of indubitable axioms replaced by provisional assumptions, the idea of subjective individual conviction replaced by public agreement within the informed community, and, finally, the notion of linear thought replaced by that of circumstantial reasoning. We have here a thorough-going attempt to make explicit the operative canons of modern experimental science, to oppose them to classical rationalism, to justify them and make them generally available, and to bring philosophical conceptions into line with them.

In "How to Make our Ideas Clear" (published, significantly, in *Popular Science Monthly* for January 1878), Peirce offers a special critique of rationalistic criteria of clarification, which supplements the arguments we have just considered. Rejecting the Cartesian appeal to the clearness and distinctness of ideas as determined by introspection, Peirce also argues that abstract definitions are radically insufficient from a scientific standpoint.

The highest grade of clarification, for Peirce, is a form of what has since become known as "operationism," a tying of ideas both to actions and to their observable effects by means of an if-then rule or "habit." To develop the meaning of an idea, "we have, therefore, simply to determine what habits it produces, for what a thing means is simply what habits it involves." Given an idea, we need to consider what effects would ensue from specified operations upon its referent. "Our conception of these effects is the whole of our conception of the object."

Educational Aims Suggested by the Pragmatic View

This summary brings us to the significance of Peirce's ideas to education, for his doctrine of meaning has an obvious message for those who would explain concepts to children. Familiarity is not enough, nor is mere verbal definition—a theme memorably amplified in James's *Talks to Teachers*. The idea needs to be concretely related to the child's actions and his expectation of consequences ensuing therefrom. This requires, in turn, opportunities for him to act and to observe the consequences of his action in a purposive context. Here is the theoretical germ of the familiar Deweyan emphasis on meaning as the perception of relations between action and consequences.

Here is the root of the "progressive" idea that teaching needs to be carried out in purposive units of action, so that subject matter takes on meaning as mediator between purposive action and observable result.

In Peirce's conception of inquiry initiated by real doubt, we have, furthermore, a major source of the problem theory of teaching, the theory that genuine thought is elicited only in the effort to overcome a genuinely felt difficulty, and that teaching should therefore be organized around problem units relevant to the situation of the students. Moreover, Peirce's conception of beliefs as habits orienting us to the future makes it evident that beliefs are always in principle subject to the test of further experience. It provides a source of the progressive emphasis on the tentative character of beliefs and on the notion that genuine inquiry provides its own intrinsic discipline. For the overcoming of doubt by attainment of belief is continually subject to the observable check of future experience. Educationally, the ideal discipline is to be conceived not as externally imposed by adults, but as flowing from the very process of meaningful inquiry in which solutions to real problems are sought.

It is important to note again that the educational suggestions inherent in Peirce's ideas were not developed by him; nor did they emerge originally from any direct intent to influence schooling. The initial motivation was theoretical, and the main goal was to spell out the general import of actual scientific standards and practices for a modern theory of knowledge. Abstract formulations such as those of Peirce nevertheless take on an autonomous life and enter into the pervasive social and intellectual climate of the educator and other thoughtful men. They filter into textbooks and explanations, they subtly alter the teacher's attitudes and conceptions of the task of schooling, and they form the basis for further philosophical criticism and interpretation, which in turn have their effects on what the school tries to do and how it proceeds. Though they do not directly address themselves to issues of practice nor provide the basis for technological development, these abstractions exercise long-run practical influence in channeling the reflective attitudes of men, attitudes which, after all, determine the uses to which technology is put.

Peirce, of course, came centuries after the initiation of modern empirical science, but he was contemporary with the beginnings of modern social and behavioral sciences, and the pragmatic viewpoint exercised significant influence on these sciences. Investigations of social problems, by such men as Quetelet and Galton, and of certain aspects of behavior, initiated by Fechner and Wundt among others, were well under way. But the methods used were almost entirely observational, descriptive, correlational, and narrowly empirical. Peirce and his successors stressed action rather than passive observation, and in psychology, education, and the biological sciences, experimental intervention came to be seen as the scientific method par excellence. Intervention in the larger social community can rarely be controlled, and experimentation has therefore played a minor role in sociology and political science. But even in such domains, and indeed in the area of social policy proper pragmatists stressed the need to be critically alert to the consequences of social action, so that we may be prepared to learn from experience whatever it can teach us. The range of critical intelligence is not to be restricted to the scope of controlled experiment, but suitably expanded so as to facilitate application to the whole realm of human conduct.

Peirce's theoretical ideas thus constituted a genuine influence on the growth of the whole series of proposals that came to be known as progressive education and that, in their more pratical formulations, have become a well-accepted part of today's prevailing view of education.

The example of historical inquiry is Frank Tracy Carlton's "Economic Influences upon Educational Progress in the United States, 1820-1850."[23]

[Carlton's work] changed the way educators viewed the rise of the public school, and in so doing affected the way they came to conceive of and participate in the development of educational policy.[24] Carlton, by sharply criticizing certain standard historical interpretations of his day, radically altered our forms of remembering, categorizing, and understanding the American education experience.

The standard interpretations of Carlton's day can be gleaned from the work of such early educational historians as Richard G. Boone, whose *Education in the United States: Its History from the Earliest Settlements* (1890) appeared in William T. Harris's influential "International Education Series," and Amory Dwight Mayo, whose majestic history of the American common school from its colonial beginnings, through Reconstruction appeared in fourteen lengthy installments in Harris's annual reports as U.S. commissioner of education. Essentially, they run as follows, though we apologize for oversimplification: The colonists came from Europe bearing a variety of traditional ideas and institutions in the realm of education; hence, the early schools and colleges in the New World tended to resemble old-world patterns. Among these patterns, the most noteworthy was the town school of Puritan New England, which offered free, equal, tax-supported education to all who desired it. After the Revolution it became clear in state after state that the new republican society would need a revised form of education if it were to survive and succeed. In response to the need, a number of heroic figures—Horace Mann in Massachusetts, Henry Barnard in Connecticut, John Pierce in Michigan, Samuel Lewis in Ohio, Caleb Mills in Indiana—worked tirelessly and selflessly in the cause of public schooling. By the Civil War, their effort had borne fruit, and public education in the New England tradition had been widely accepted in the North, the West, and parts of the South. With the defeat of the South in 1865, that acceptance soon became universal . . . .

Economic Interests as a Force in Educational Policy

Carlton's thesis was forthrightly presented, extensively documented, and strikingly original. In place of the "great man" interpretation that had cast Mann, Barnard, Pierce, Lewis, and Mills as the prime movers in the public-school movement, Carlton portrayed the educational revival between 1820 and 1850 as one phase of a larger social development, contending that (1) "the tax-supported school system evolved out of heterogeneity of population, improvement in methods of production, the specialization of industry, the division of labor, the growth of factories and the separation of homelife from industrial occupations";[25] (2) the public school system was "the resultant of the conflict of interests—economic, social, religious, and racial—within the different states";[26] and (3) "the cities and the working classes were chiefly instrumental in placing our schools upon a tax-supported basis."[27] With respect to public policy for his own time, Carlton drew a clear moral: social forces, not altruistic leaders, had been and would continue to be the decisive factors in American educational progress. "If generalization is warranted by the data before us," Carlton counseled, "the conclusion is warranted that, in modern times, the trend of educational advance is determined by economic evolution. On the one hand, the student of educational problems, who is striving to improve the work of the public schools, must study the trend of industrial and social evolution; and, on the other hand, the political economist and social scientists must consider the economic and social signif- of uniform advance in educational and industrial evolution."[28]

For all its boldness and originality, Carlton's monograph elicited surprisingly little comment when it first appeared; one searches the learned journals in vain for anything more than passing notice. But the monograph did exert profound influence on subsequent scholarship. In 1910, John Commons and Helen Sumner gave the monograph unqualified endorsement in the monumental *Documentary History of American Industrial Society;* and eight years later, this endorsement was repeated in the *History of Labour in the United States,* which quickly established itself as the standard work in its field. Carlton himself restated his theses in *Organized Labor in American History* (1920) and in numerous other of his works in labor history and economics.

More to the point of our report, Carlton deeply affected the thought of Ellwood P. Cubberley, a Stanford professor of education whose *Public Education in the United States* (1919; revised, 1934) was a most influential work. Indeed, Carlton's impact on Cubberley must be judged decisive, not only with respect to the crucial matter of periodization, but also with respect to the seven celebrated "battles" for free public education that have long been associated with Cubberley's work. At the very least, Cubberley borrowed from Carlton the idea of an "alignment of interests" for and against tax-supported education; and he followed Carlton in relating these interests and arguments to the social, political, and economic changes that marked American life in the first half of the nineteenth century. Mann, Barnard, and the others still parade through the pages of Cubberley's book, but there is no mistaking the dramatic difference between Cubberley's interpretation and those that had come before: educational policy making was now portrayed as a political process— a series of conflicts or battles—that took place within the context of a larger social evolution. Men still acted but they acted as the representatives of social, religious, and ethnic interests. And the outcome of the battles was clearly conditioned by the social realities of the time.

Effects on the Thinking of Schoolmen

The interpretation proffered by Carlton and Cubberley gave American schoolmen in the 1920s, 1930s, and 1940s a much more sophisticated view of how American educational policy had been made in the past and how it was being made in their own time. In place of heroes, they were directed to political and social processes as the crucial factors in educational change, a shift that doubtless prepared them more effectively for the realities of their situation. And in place of small-town America, they were directed to the cities, and more particularly, to the aspiring workingmen within the cities, as the source of much that was characteristic and distinctive in the idea and practice of universal public education.

Yet granted this, the interpretation of Carlton and Cubberley also served to put blinders on the schoolmen of the generation between the two world wars. For one thing, Carlton's conceptualization of political interest groups was at many points vague and incomplete. He included among those supporting public schools a category called "citizens of the Republic," and among those opposing public schools, a category called "taxpayers"; both categories, of course, so imprecise as to be worthless. Furthermore, Carlton tended to accept the public statements of the various interest groups at face value and failed to look beyond to the behavior of these groups in elections and in legislatures. Had he done so, he would have found that the workingmen were less than consistent in their support of public schooling, while businessmen, who are not mentioned at all in the alignment of interest, were often in the vanguard of the movement.

Even more important, perhaps, was the use to which Cubberley put Carlton's analysis in arguing that the great battles for public education had been won, and that, from the 1880s on, the primary problem facing Americans was to improve and refine their school system. Nurtured on this interpretation, many schoolmen of the 1940s and 1950s were simply at a loss to understand the criticisms of public education that came to the fore during the postwar era. Equipped with an inadequate version of the political history of American education, mistaking a particular coalition of interests that had won a particular set of nineteenth-century battles for some fictitious permanent coalition that had won some sort of epochal conflict for all time, they found themselves unable to comprehend the criticisms directed against them and unable to muster the political strength they needed to defend their programs. Partly as a result, they ended up impugning the motives of their critics instead of responding to their charges.

Finally, there was the implicit Darwinism of the Carlton and Cubberley interpretation, which asserted that "in modern times, the trend of educational advance is determined by economic evolution." Had both men taken their argument seriously—and to do so would have raised grave questions about the significance of the great "battles" they so dramatically portrayed—they would have considered not merely the uniqueness of the American educational experience, but also its basic similarity to that of other industrializing nations. Had they done that, they might have equipped educators of the 1950s to realize that the educational crises of that era were the result neither of a conspiracy nor of a failure, but rather of the relentless pressure of a developing technology on the social ingenuity of men.

These extended excerpts from the committee report have been included in this volume because they furnish both a background of the emergence and direction of educational research in the past and a description of the way in which several types of research have influenced the thinking and practice of education.

Except for the brief comments on laboratory schools, these quotations do not give the reader information about the changing character of educational development. The laboratory schools have played a significant role in educational development. Instructional materials and systems of instruction have been developed in them. For example, the series of textbooks in the social studies produced largely in the Lincoln School of Teachers College, Columbia University, by Harold Rugg and his colleagues had a wide sale in a large number of schools in the 1930s and 1940s. The so-called "Look-Say" readers were developed largely in the laboratory schools of the University of Chicago, as were the Freeman Handwriting System and the Morrison Unit Plan of instruction. The University Elementary School of the University of California, Los Angeles, was central in the development of ungraded classrooms. Progressive schools not connected with universities also served in the development of instructional systems and materials; those of the Winnetka, Illinois, schools and of the Dalton School in New York City are among the best known. Some early educational reformers like Pestalozzi, Herbart, and Montessori developed systems of learning and instructional materials as necessary parts of the schools they created.

College and university professors in America, working in conjunction with publishers, have been, however, the chief agents of educational development since the time of McGuffey and his famous readers. Professors of education, through their work in the preparation of elementary and secondary school teachers, have been the main developers of instructional systems, often in collaboration with cooperating schools and teachers. For example, the common methods used in the United States for the teaching of reading, arithmetic, social studies, spelling, handwriting, and composition were all developed under the leadership of professors of education.

In some cases, the extent of disciplined inquiry that has gone into these developments has been reported, particularly in the trial and testing periods in the development of instructional materials. Usually, however, no reports are available to appraise the kind and quality of development activities in the field of education. Furthermore, most college professors and teachers do not keep an accurate record of the time and effort they devote to these activities. Hence, we can only make very crude estimates of the costs of development that are involved when the work is done by professors and teachers outside of their regular teaching responsibilities.

Somewhat more dependable estimates are available regarding the funds spent in the United States on the development of instructional materials by educational publishers. At present, approximately 1.5 percent of the operating budgets of elementary and secondary schools is used to purchase instructional materials, a total annual cost of $900,000,000. Educational publishers vary among themselves in terms of the proportion of their income devoted to development, but the average is reported to be 10 percent. This means that they spend approximately $90,000,000 annually on the development of instructional materials.

During recent years some school systems have encouraged teachers and other staff members to develop instructional materials designed particularly for local needs. There has been support of workshops in which the chief purpose is to enable the participants to develop needed instructional materials. Expenditures for this type of development have probably exceeded those of the commercial publishers. It is reasonable to conclude, therefore, that in the immediate past the total direct and indirect expenditures for development made by local schools and individual authors and designers have been far greater than those supplied for this purpose by the federal government. We need to know more about the quality, effectiveness, and efficiency of the development efforts in order to suggest the directions for improvement in the future.

Quality refers to the nature of the inquiry that is carried on as the design, construction, and testing of the system or the product proceeds. Effectiveness concerns the results from the use of the system or product in terms of the improvements in students' learning. Efficiency relates to the relative cost per pupil or other appropriate unit of use. The prevailing practice, in which schools or teachers select the products they wish to use, is likely to result in greater effectiveness and efficiency of commercial products than those where the user has little to say regarding their production. But neither procedure guarantees the quality of the development activities. The prospects of educational development are partly dependent on the working out of procedures that maximize quality, effectiveness, and efficiency. Recent development projects supported by federal funds vary widely in quality, have generally been no better than average in effectiveness, and have been low in efficiency.

The history of educational development in the United States has reflected the prevailing concerns of educational improvement and reform. Until Sputnik stimulated federal funds for national curriculum projects, the pattern of support remained largely unchanged. The proportion of federal support reached its peak in 1973, representing at that time perhaps 25 percent of the total funds expended. The future directions of both research and development are not clearly indicated by their past history.

Notes

1. *Research for Tomorrow's Schools*, ed. Lee Cronbach and Patrick Suppes (New York: Macmillan, 1969), 42.

2. *Ibid.*, 43-48.

3. J. M. Rice, *The Public School System of the United States* (New York: Century Co., 1893).

4. William James, *Talks to Teachers on Psychology* (New York: Holt, 1920), 7-11.

5. Leonard P. Ayres, "History and Present Status of Educational Measurements," in *The Measurement of Educational Products*, ed. Guy M. Whipple, Seventeenth Yearbook of the National Society for the Study of Education, Part II (Bloomington, Ill.: Public School Publishing Co., 1918), 9-15.

6. Raymond E. Callahan, *Education and the Cult of Efficiency* (Chicago: Phoenix, 1964).

7. Walter S. Monroe, "Existing Tests and Standards," in *The Measurement of Educational Products*, ed. Whipple, 71-104.

8. *Research for Tomorrow's Schools*, ed. Cronbach and Suppes, 49-51.

9. John Dewey, "Criticisms Wise and Otherwise on Modern Child Study," National Educational Association, *Proceedings and Addresses* 36 (1897): 867-868.

10. John Dewey, "The University School," *University Record* 1 (1896): 417-419.

11. *Ibid.*

12. Quoted in *Dewey on Education,* ed. Martin S. Dworkin (New York: Bureau of Publications, Teachers College, Columbia University, 1959), 90.

13. *Research for Tomorrow's Schools,* ed. Cronbach and Suppes, 59-61.

14. Howard M. Jones, Frances Keppel, and Robert Ulich, "On the Conflict between the 'Liberal Arts' and the 'Schools of Education,' " *ACLS Newsletter* 5 (No. 2, 1954): 17-38.

15. Nicholas Murray Butler, *Across the Busy Years,* Vol. I (New York: Charles Scribner's Sons, 1939), 86.

16. T. R. McConnell, "The Nature of Educational Research," in *The Conceptual Structure of Educational Research,* Supplementary Educational Monographs No. 55 (Chicago: University of Chicago, 1942), 1-21.

17. *Research for Tomorrow's Schools,* ed. Cronbach and Suppes, 66-68.

18. Dean Chamberlin *et al., Did They Succeed in College?* (New York: Harper, 1942).

19. Henry Chauncey, "Some Observations on Evaluation in the Eight-Year Study," *North Central Association Quarterly* 15 (January 1941): 257-264; Helmer G. Johnson, "Weakness in the Eight-Year Study," *School and Society* 63 (June 15, 1946): 417-419.

20. Abraham Shumsky, *The Action Research Way of Learning* (New York: Teachers College, 1958), 94.

21. *Research for Tomorrow's Schools,* ed. Cronbach and Suppes, 89-95.

22. Charles Sanders Peirce, "Some Consequences of Four Incapacities," *Journal of Speculative Philosophy* 2 (No. 3, 1868): 140-157.

23. *Research for Tomorrow's Schools,* ed. Cronbach and Suppes, 111-118.

24. Frank Tracy Carlton, *Economic Influences upon Educational Progress in the United States, 1820-1850* (New York: Teachers College Press, 1965). The original edition of this work was published in 1908 by the University of Wisconsin.

25. *Ibid.,* 130.

26. *Ibid.,* 83.

27. *Ibid.,* 134-135.

28. *Ibid.,* 144-145.

3. POLITICAL PROBLEMS IN OBTAINING FEDERAL SUPPORT

The initial authorization of federal funds to support educational research was PL 531, the Cooperative Research Act, passed by the Congress in 1954. The fact that such a bill was introduced and enacted is largely due to the intelligent planning and persuasion of Samuel Brownell, U.S. commissioner of education, and the active interest in research of the late Congressman John Fogarty. However, the first appropriation under this act was not made until 1957. It was for less than $1,000,000, two-thirds of which was for research on the educational problems of the mentally retarded, an area of interest of a number of influential members of Congress. Obtaining federal support was not easy, and the initial funds were small. Sputnik stimulated national concern regarding the effectiveness of education in comparison to the Soviet Union, particularly in such fields as science, mathematics, and foreign languages, which were viewed as necessities in maintaining this country's defense against aggression. This resulted in the enactment of the National Defense Education Act of 1958, which authorized educational research and development in certain fields, large appropriations for the National Science Foundation to use in efforts to improve science education, and sharply increased appropriations for the Cooperative Research Program. In 1965 the Elementary and Secondary Education Act was passed. Its Title IV expanded the authority of the Office of Education in research and included explicit authorization for research and development centers, which had been supported for two years under the implicit authority of the Office of Education, *and for the support of education laboratories to help schools develop and utilize educational research in attacking their problems. The groundwork was laid for a comprehensive program for federal participation in all aspects of educational research and development. For three years appropriations increased. The educational research community thus believed that the federal government was to be not only the chief source of funds but also an increasingly adequate source. By 1969, however, the increased appropriations for the network of laboratories and research and development centers were much smaller than these institutions had expected and for which they had planned. Furthermore, the unsolicited research funds on which most university faculty members depended were diminishing. By 1974 half of the laboratories and research centers were in the process of dissolution or were planning for very serious reductions in programs. Funds for the support of unsolicited research proposals had shrunk still further. This situation not only focused attention on the political problems involved in getting federal support, but also raised the more general question concerning prospects for future educational research and development.*

In 1971 Sidney Marland, then commissioner of education, expressed the view that some of the difficult political problems would be eliminated by the establishment of the National Institute of Education.[1]

A recent witness at a House subcommittee hearing on the National Institute of Education expressed his conviction that federally sponsored educational research and development would be far more productive if it were removed from Office of Education jurisdiction and placed in the NIE. In a federal agency such as the USOE, he reasoned, interests change from commissioner to commissioner; and experimental failure, the quintessence of the research route to invention, tends to become unacceptable in the vagaries of bureaucratic life.

I am not persuaded that the Office of Education sheds more darkness than light in the land, and yet I agree with his point. If educational research and development is going to be the success it really must be in this country, then it cannot exist in the compromised anonymity of the conventional federal bureaucracy. The time has clearly come, as President Nixon proposes, to establish a focus for educational research and experimentation in the United States. To achieve a genuine impact on education's problems, we must create the setting and the atmosphere in which the crucial and delicate work of research and development can thrive, funded generously, isolated from political and administrative whim, and dedicated to one purpose alone—the discovery and application of new alternatives in education.

First, the National Institute of Education will be a separate agency within HEW, detached from the Office of Education. It will report through the commissioner of education to the secretary of HEW. The NIE will be responsible for the planning and direction of research and development at all levels of schooling, while the USOE will administer operational programs, as it does now. The USOE will, furthermore, be strongly linked with the NIE for the necessary input of ideas and needs, and for the follow-up dissemination of NIE products.

The director of the institute will be a presidential appointee, according the position the status to recruit a national figure, commanding the respect to attract the very best scientists, educational practitioners, public administrators, and others essential to the high importance of the NIE. Above all, the NIE's director must be capable of developing solutions to pressing educational problems. He need not be overly concerned with administration and congressional relations because these are areas in which the secretary of HEW and the commissioner of education can play a strong supportive role for the NIE without cluttering its affairs with unnecessary governmental restraints.

The director will be assisted by a National Advisory Council on Research and Development. The council will be involved in setting general policy for the NIE and in coordinating its efforts with outside agencies such as the National Science Foundation, the Office of Economic Opportunity, the National Institute of Mental Health, the Office of Child Development, and so on. Some personnel would rotate from the NIE to the Office of Education and back again to maintain close cooperation between the two sister agencies, bringing real world experience to NIE planning and a high level of knowledge and motivation to the operations of the USOE.

At least two kinds of functioning groups will exist within the institute—task forces addressing major problems, and study groups seeking to understand the nature of the processes of education at a deeper level. Both will consist of permanent NIE staff people, plus outside consultants and short-term fellows of the institute.

Two parallel efforts will supplement the task forces and study groups—an intramural program of research and development, and a researcher training program operating through institutes, fellowships, and training contracts.

However the staff is organized, certain personnel patterns character-istic of learning research and development agencies will emerge. These distinctive patterns will be made possible in large part by the NIE's authority to hire and compensate technical and professional staff exempt from civil service classification and compensation regulations. This authority, I should stress, will only apply when there is a specific reason to use it; hence very likely many of the staff members will be hired under the civil service system. The special authority is not likely to be used for those engaged in support functions for the agency, such as budget, personnel, and contracts.

The concept of civil service exemption authority builds upon the experience of other successful research and development institutions, such as the National Science Foundation and the National Institutes of Health. As these agencies have found, drawing the highest quality staff for research and development requires staffing patterns and compensation levels specially adapted to the career patterns and professional traditions of the scholarly community. Exemption permits, for example, a system of short-term, noncareer appoint-ments. Distinguished academicians and educators whose permanent career commitment is to a university, school system, or industry could join the NIE staff for even shorter periods to work on a single project. In addition, the authority would permit streamlined hiring procedures particularly suited for short-term, high-level personnel.

With flexibility in recruiting and the ability to pay salaries com-mensurate with the type of talent that is sought, we hope to attract to the NIE the most significant names in education. But beyond our distinguished colleagues in education, we would also expect to attract their counterparts from many other disciplines such as sociology, biochemistry, psychiatry, medicine, anthropology, and so on.

What will these scholars and academicians do at the NIE? This question is presently absorbing the attention of a good many thinkers and planners, and we feel a broad pattern of priorities is emerging from these deliberations, the principal areas to which the fully functioning NIE will address its organized talents.

Let me stress that such speculation in no way implies limiting the scope of the organization. In truth, as we envision the NIE, the entire universe of educational concerns will be its concern. The NIE will have the range of capabilities required to match the wonderfully varied, endlessly changing, hundred-sided activities of education. It will deal with concrete problems such as education of the disadvantaged, career education, and higher education. But the men and women of the NIE will not be harnessed to immediacy; their purpose will be as broad as the very nature of learning itself. They will look deeply into the learning process in all its physical, biological, and psychological aspects, to explore in an unfettered atmosphere of pure investigation the far reaches of man's capacity to create knowledge and transmit it. The knowledge base upon which education now rests, our ablest scholars agree, is still in its infancy. We propose to increase it systematically.

More concretely, I would like to sketch for you briefly some of the objectives and plans we have in mind in establishing the institute.

First, it will seek new knowledge and new insights into educational experience. It will do basic research into the learning process in all its sociological and physiological variables. We will want to undertake studies that may not lead to immediate changes in practice, such as the examination of the effects of chemical stimulation upon learning, as well as studies that are likely immediately to influence present policy and practice. The institute will certainly be concerned with increasing the productivity of teachers; it will look for ways to utilize technology to enhance the teacher's life; it will look for ways to make education available and deliverable to all who want it, whatever their circumstances.

Second, the NIE will seek useful alternatives in educational practice in order to offer the people of this country a far wider range of new procedures, new operations, and new products than they presently enjoy. One choice in anything is simply not enough. An elementary school curriculum that works perfectly well in Boston, for example, could be wholly incorrect, ineffective, and perhaps even damaging in San Antonio, Texas. And we must recognize in our schools, at every level, that there is no single ladder for individual fulfillment and success. If boys who love to fix cars are becoming unhappy office managers, somebody is wasting money, talent, and happiness—precious commodities that we waste at our individual and collective peril. We have much to learn about human needs and the capacity of our institutions of learning to help their individuals meet those needs.

Administrative and management issues and problems will be apt topics for the NIE's investigation as we try to establish closer ties between the costs of education and its beneficiaries. For example, we could conceivably develop and extend to the entire nation a plan such as the one Ohio State University will soon begin operating in which students will be allowed to pay for college out of the future earnings of all students. Or perhaps business and industry could assume a specific new tax for higher education, a talent tax that corresponds to the number of college graduates annually engaged.

Third, we see the institute strengthening the nation's research and development capability through the stimulation and training of new scholars. The new respectability of educational research will, I believe, greatly increase the number of competent professional persons engaged in the field. Even in the unlikely event of Congress's appropriating a billion dollars this year for educational research and development, expenditure of such a huge sum, while compatible with other fields of research, might actually cause more harm than good because there are not enough competent people to do the work at this level of investment. And even if we were able to collect together all the talented people in this country who would like nothing better than to work for the improvement of education, we have neither the organization nor the network of communications to absorb their efforts fruitfully.

The NIE will take the responsibility for coordinating educational research and development efforts throughout the entire federal government, as well as for providing general leadership and support to training now taking place within universities and laboratories. The institute will also administer grants, institutes, and fellowships as methods of supporting and encouraging the growth of competence in people committed to educational research and development.

Fourth, the institute will undertake the invention and perfection of ways to deliver educational innovations we know are successful. Whatever sort of breakthrough we achieve in teaching and learning, it will be useless unless it is linked with a system for delivery that works. That is why I maintain that the NIE holds the genius of that central system, flowing collegially, constructively, and systematically through the education network into the classrooms of America. Systematizing the art and science of teaching is one of the principal reasons for the NIE. The art and science of teaching are very human things, changing with the people affected and with the time and place. The NIE must be, more than ordinarily, a humane institution.

We know there are many sound innovations in education, methods that have proved their effectiveness over and over again. I refer to such techniques as peer tutoring, individual progress programs, and the use of paraprofessionals in the classroom. But we also know that too many school systems are skilled at protecting themselves from the invasion of good ideas, and, as a consequence, good techniques such as those I just alluded to—and many more—are serving only a fraction of the schoolchildren of this nation, illuminating only a fraction of the darkness.

The NIE's dissemination efforts will build upon and utilize the facilities and experience of the National Center for Educational Communication, the Office of Education's dissemination arm, and other delivery systems. Parallel with the growth of the NIE, I see a reshaping of the total commitment of the Office of Education to accelerating nationwide use of tested educational improvements resulting from NIE and other efforts. We can no longer accept a situation in which we can deliver a new mouthwash to 200,000,000 Americans in a matter of weeks while a new system of education to freshen the quality of our minds moves with glacial imperceptibility. The dissemination of the NIE's products and processes is one of the principal reasons for the close articulation with the USOE and its vast human network of states, local systems, and classrooms.

To summarize our thinking about the role of the NIE, we believe that the lion's share of the agency's budget would be devoted to mobilizing the ablest scholars and directing their talents to comprehensive research and development programs seeking solutions to education's most serious problems. Some of these solutions will build on the best current techniques—and many will probe radically new approaches to learning. All will lean heavily on development and on the invention of effective means of translating ideas into readily deliverable materials and practices which are workable—and working—in the field. The institute's independent, creative atmosphere and flexible organization will enable its staff to take a hard look at the common assumptions and hallowed traditions of the profession and exposed us to ourselves where we are found wanting, suggesting solutions.

Teams of people with different expertise—research and development personnel, educators, teachers, public officials, engineers, economists, statisticians, artists—will be organized around basic problems. They will plan research and development programs designed to yield new knowledge, materials, and methods and coordinated to provide powerful leverage on each problem. For example, finding successful approaches to educating the disadvantaged might mean supporting a range of projects from basic language studies to designing alternatives to formal schooling for alienated ghetto teenagers.

As many of you know, when I became commissioner in December several new staff members joined me in the Office of Education. Among them is Harry Silberman, director of the National Center for Educational Research and Development, the Office of Education's present research operation. A principal concern of his has been to reorganize the NCERD in preparation for transfer of most of its functions to the institute while continuing to operate the USOE research and development effort until the NIE becomes a reality. Silberman is already assembling able and lively people to reinforce the NCERD-NIE component during this period of development.

The NIE must be responsive to the Office of Education's role in serving American education broadly. The Office of Education, for its part, must be in a position to help formulate the questions the NIE would address. Further, the USOE must strengthen and expand the delivery system for promoting implementation of the practical results of educational research and development in the field. There is a large new role for the USOE in this context which I call leadership and some call technical assistance. Stated simply, it is that a new idea will be delivered and sustained not only by memorandums and journal articles but by people on call.

To summarize, the NIE would assume most activities now conducted by the National Center for Educational Research and Development. The NIE would become responsible for programs in basic research, ongoing development activities, the research and development centers and regional education laboratories, research training, and construction of research and development facilities.

The Office of Education would retain its responsibility for evaluation and policy-oriented research relating to USOE programs and the gathering and dissemination of statistics. While the NIE would be charged with designing new delivery systems for research products, the USOE would oversee demonstration and dissemination activities and support and deploy whatever new system the NIE might develop.

We look to the NIE to bridge the education and related research and development activities of all federal agencies, activities largely unconnected at the moment. The NIE would act as a clearinghouse for information on relevant programs and provide an intellectual meeting ground where personnel of various government agencies can reason together about educational problems, supporting each other, avoiding duplication and cross-purposes. For example, extraordinary institutional materials have been developed by the Department of Defense. No systematic arrangement exists for their adaptation and articulation in the school system of the country.

At the time Marland wrote, he had no inkling of the serious political problems NIE would face. Lindley Stiles, on the other hand, has long been interested in the political process as it operates on educational matters. He was one of the earliest educational leaders to recognize the political problems involved in getting support for the Cooperative Research Program. He published an interesting account of his own experiences in the Journal of Educational Research.[2]

A Historical Note

The first efforts to establish a research component for education came with the passage, in 1954, of the Cooperative Research Act by the federal government. This legislation was developed under the leadership of Dr. Samuel Brownell, commissioner of education, and spearheaded through the Congress by the late Congressman John Fogarty of Rhode Island. In 1957, it received its first appropriation, $500,000, all earmarked for research on mental retardation, a special concern of Congressman Fogarty and a purpose for which public opinion could be motivated. The appropriation passed, as I later learned from Congressman Fogarty, without any visible support from the education community. Interest in research was so low at that time, in fact, that officials of the U.S. Office of Education had to make personal appeals to deans of schools of education across the country to get them to persuade professors to develop research programs in this area. A key reason for the inept response of the research community was the relatively few trained educational researchers in the country—only about 150, half of whom were employed by one agency, the Educational Testing Service. Other causes, I found at Wisconsin, were a reluctance of professors to give up the security of full-time teaching assignments for short-term research commitments and a general disinterest in the problems of mental retardation. Nevertheless, after intensive efforts by a few deans of education and professors (I wrote two proposals myself and then found professors to work on them) the $500,000 appropriation was invested in research. A year later, the appropriation was increased to $1,000,000 with three-fourths of the amount earmarked for the study of mental retardation and the rest available for research on other kinds of educational problems. Again the appropriation was passed with little support from educators across the country; Congressman Fogarty, who deserves credit for the involvement of the federal government in support for educational research, was its major champion.

A million dollars is not very much money, as governmental appropriations go, but it was enough to attract the attention of bureaucrats in the Office of Education. Shortly after this appropriation was passed, I learned that a move was under way in that office to allocate the research funds for personnel in the various departments instead of to research in universities and state departments of education across the country. Such would be easily accomplished inasmuch as the Congress had neglected to give educational research a line item in the Office of Education budget. I wrote immediately to Commissioner Lawrence Derthick (Brownell's successor) protesting such contemplated action and sent copies of my letter to a number of deans and chief state school officers whom I knew to be interested in the research program and urged them to make their views known to the commissioner. Many did. The expression of support for the research program led Commissioner Derthick, who had been unaware of the contemplated transfer of funds, to pledge that the research appropriation would be protected. Nevertheless, this near loss of federal funds for research made me and others realize that more vigorous and widespread support from the field would be essential if the federal government's investment in educational research was to be protected and expanded. Such feelings were intensified the next year, 1959, after the appropriation had been doubled again to $2,000,000, when I learned that federal budget makers were proposing to eliminate appropriations for educational research entirely on the grounds that funds already expended in this area were sufficient to solve all educational problems.

During the first two years of the Cooperative Research Program a number of deans of education and state superintendents of public instruction, primarily those whose organizations had already received research grants, had worked individually with Office of Education officials to encourage larger budget requests for research. Commissioner Derthick and Dr. Roy Hall, director of the Cooperative Research Program, were sympathetic but unable to break the pattern of percentage budget increases maintained by the Bureau of the Budget. It was becoming increasingly clear that if any substantial increases in the appropriations for research were to be achieved, we would have to work directly with Congress. At the same time, we did not want to bypass the efforts of leaders in the Office of Education. Consequently, in October of 1960, I assembled a group of eight deans of education,[3] drawn from representative public and nonpublic universities from different regions of the nation, to meet with Commissioner Derthick, Dr. Hall, and other key staff members of the Office of Education. At this historic meeting, we agreed that substantially larger appropriations for educational research should be sought by direct approaches to Congress and that each member of the deans' group would endeavor to promote wide-scale contacts with congressional leaders in his own region. To facilitate the effort, I volunteered to serve as coordinator of ideas and information as well as to organize contacts with congressional committees, functions I have been fulfilling ever since.[4] Each dean agreed to send me the names of educational leaders who were willing to work for federal research appropriations. Subsequently, I developed a mailing list of Volunteers for Educational Research[5] and endeavored to keep everyone informed about legislative and budget matters, with sufficient lead time to act.[6] I also began organizing teams of educational leaders—deans, state superintendents, superintendents of schools, and school board members, as well as researchers—to appear at congressional committee hearings when budgets and policies for educational research and development were considered.[7]

Our efforts to promote support for educational research were saturated with both frustrating and satisfying experiences. We learned early that most educators did not really believe in research; they simply were not oriented to the scientific approach. In contrast to the general disinterest of educators, we found that many congressmen were sensitive to what research had done in other fields and believed that it could help education as well. They welcomed our help and eagerly sought to make a strong case for increases in federal investments in research to improve schools. We discovered, too, that budgets for federal activities are made as much or more in appropriations committees as they are by agency recommendations and Bureau of the Budget actions. Policies for research tend to follow appropriations. As we learned more about how public policy evolves and the forces that set priorities for congressional attention, we realized that individual congressmen strive diligently to represent their clients. They have many demands on their attention and efforts; the natural tendency is to respond to those that appear to be most persistent and most wanted by their constituents back home. An appropriation that has no strong constituency behind it has little chance of winning support. In addition, no matter how much the chairman and members of a congressional committee may favor a recommendation, it has little chance of passing the House or Senate unless a solid case is built for it—in hearing testimony, in papers submitted for the record by professional experts, and in letters and telegrams from interested constituents. Above all, we discovered that the best kind of communication with one's representatives or senators is based on personal acquaintance. In our efforts we were constantly reminded of the old political adage which runs: a politician cannot help anybody unless he gets elected. Hence, we tried to let the people in a congressman's district know what he or she was doing to support educational research.

On the frustrating side, we already knew when we decided to organize a group of volunteers that professional organizations would not support legislation or appropriations in this area, partly because some did not really endorse research as a means of improving schools but more generally because all were afraid of losing their tax-exempt status. The National Education Association (NEA) and its powerful subsidiary body, the American Association of School Administrators, refused to support appropriations for educational research until the passage of the Elementary and Secondary Education Act in 1965, which they were finally persuaded to support by a personal appeal from President Lyndon Johnson, because they were against "categorical aid." The American Association of Colleges for Teacher Education did enact resolutions in support of appropriations, and many deans who were members worked as volunteers, but the association itself devoted little staff time to organizing support. Our biggest disappointment came when the American Educational Research Association (AERA), which should have taken the lead, instead frittered away its energies debating whether federal involvement in research was a good idea, the merits of researcher versus mission-oriented research, and the question of who was making policy for educational research. Not until 1969 did the AERA finally authorize its staff to become active in organizing support for research legislation and appropriations.[8]

In retrospect, it is understandable that many educational leaders and professional organizations had little dedication to research on educational problems and were reluctant to become involved in the democratic processes by which public policy is developed. Research had yet to prove itself, and politics was a dirty word to many educators. Even among those who supported educational research appropriations, it was frustrating to deal with the lack of vision that prevailed with respect to what a genuine research and development component for education should be. I recall a comment by one dean of a well-known school of education that is illustrative of the kind of shortsightedness that was common. I had proposed that the $2,000,000 appropriation of 1959 be increased to $25,000,000 the next year. In a shocked voice he cried, "No, No, Lin, all we need is about $2,000,000 a year more—ever."

As I left the meeting in which this comment was voiced, I expressed my frustration to my old friend Dr. Wayne Reid, associate commissioner of education, by asking him if we could not find someone to help us who could think in terms of hundreds of millions for educational research rather than at the token level that educators were willing to accept. Two weeks later, I received a call from Dr. Reid telling me that I was going to be invited to become a member of the Advisory Committee of the Aerospace Education Foundation of the Air Force Association. His advice was: "Accept the invitation; this is a group that knows what research can do, is aware that R and D requires substantial investments, and most importantly, can exert powerful influence on the Congress." It was the best advice that I have ever taken for educational research. At the first meeting of the foundation's Executive Committee after I came onto its Advisory Committee, the group heard our story and immediately authorized its staff to give all possible support. Since that time, under the astute leadership of James Straubel, executive secretary, the association has enlisted the support of prominent business, scientific, industrial, and defense leaders in support of legislation and appropriations for educational research. The partnership they have helped to mold among these key groups has become not only a strong force for research but also for the improvement and redirection of all of education.

All members of the Volunteers for Educational Research have personal anecdotes to tell of their experiences in winning the support of representatives and senators for educational research. In one state, a senator who had previously led the fight *against* appropriations was persuaded to reverse his position and fight instead for an increase in the budget in Joint Conference Committee. A key victory in Wisconsin was the decision of Congressman Melvin Laird (now Secretary of Defense) to give active leadership for legislation and appropriations for educational research. Laird, a Republican, joined with Fogarty, a Democrat, on the Subcommittee of the House Education and Labor Committee (where appropriations for the Office of Education originate) to build bipartisan support. He personally wrote the legislation that gave educational research its own line item in the Office of Education budget; such improvements as the provision of funds to train educational researchers; creation of the small-grant program; the opening of research to school systems, state departments of education, and the education industries as well as institutions of higher learning; and the requirement that research proposals be evaluated by panels of independent professionals. When the Hall of Fame for Educational Research is established, Melvin Laird deserves to stand along with John Fogarty and Jim Straubel as one who also fought the fight to develop a research component for education.

The efforts of the Volunteers for Educational Research, which included lay as well as professional leaders, have been quietly effective in helping to pass a number of pieces of key legislation. They achieved the establishment of the research center program in institutions of higher learning, under President John F. Kennedy.[9] They helped to pass the Elementary and Secondary Education Act, which included the Cooperative Research Program under Title IV and provisions for the Regional Research Laboratories, under President Johnson.[10] They helped to pass the Higher Education Act, legislation for mental retardation and vocational education research and development, and helped to maintain appropriations for the National Science Foundation and the National Defense Education Act. Most of these gains were made during the time that Dr. Francis Keppel served as commissioner of education. He, along with the associate commissioner for research, Dr. Ralph Flynt, a most astute politician, and the assistant commissioner for research, Dr. Francis A. J. Ianni, provided vigorous leadership in advancing proposals and increasing budget requests for educational research, which the volunteers helped to move through the Congress. All three of these men belong in the Educational Research Hall of Fame with Fogarty, Laird, and Straubel. They gave leadership to achieving breakthroughs for educational research when the going was hardest.[11]

More recently, the volunteers have worked to achieve the passage of legislation to establish a national institute for education. The idea is to give to education a program of research and development similar in function and level of support to the institutes' very successful program in the field of health. Key objectives are to keep research free from partisan politics and to provide concentrations of resources to correct critical educational weaknesses. Impetus for the institute legislation comes from the support given by President Nixon and the strong backing of Dr. Sidney Marland, commissioner of education. Congressman John Brademas of Indiana, a Democrat, has spearheaded the bipartisan legislative effort. Politically, the challenge is to establish the institute program as a new and additional thrust for research rather than merely a consolidation of existing programs under a new name. Efforts to accomplish this objective are hampered by the lack of a strong constituency for educational research, and the charges by some politicians and educational leaders that money invested in educational research is being wasted.[12] Still lingering, too, is the basic question in the minds of many about whether research (scientific inquiry) can provide the basis for the improvement of instruction in education.[13]

Stage of Development

All who have worked to establish a research component for education, and particularly those volunteers who have spearheaded efforts for legislation and appropriations, deserve to take satisfaction from achievements to date. The Cooperative Research Program and its successor in the U.S. Office of Education, the National Center for Educational Research and Development, have been able to establish a systematic program of mission-oriented research directed toward improving education at all levels.[14] The federal investment in educational research, counting all programs including those such as Headstart, has risen over a fifteen-year period from practically nothing to over $200,000,000 a year.[15] Funds for training programs have prepared a new generation of researchers, much more sophisticated and skilled, and generally committed to studying the critical educational problems in accordance with priorities set by the society rather than individual researcher preference. Fifteen hundred young researchers have been supported in graduate study, and another 10,000 have received in-service training. What is more, educational research and development is coming to be an interdisciplinary process with scholars from other fields adding their scholarly resources to the endeavor.

Federal involvement in educational research now brings support to seventeen research centers operated by universities. Nine of these are studying general problems of learning, teaching, and educational operations; four are researching ways to improve the education of handicapped children; two are concerned with vocational education; and two are developing policy for education. To translate the results of research done in the various centers into practice, eleven regional laboratories are being supported. Each of these unites in its service area the resources of schools, colleges, state departments of education, and the education industries to improve schools. The dissemination of research results is now the function of a national Educational Resources Information Center (ERIC). A small grant program administered regionally by the Office of Education is adding knowledge to the stockpiles that are required for major educational breakthroughs. At this writing, it seems probable that the national institute for education ultimately will become a reality which will bring additional resources and coordination to educational research and development efforts.

A number of recent appraisals of the educational research and development program in the United States attest to the progress that has been achieved.[16] Clearly, the federal government has become a partner with schools, colleges, and state departments of education in efforts to create a research component for education. Some evidence can be found, also, to suggest that the image of educational research is changing.[17] The "theory into practice" pattern in school improvement gradually is being displaced by the "theory to research and development to practice" processes. Teachers and school administrators, as well as professors of education, and professionals in state departments of education and the general public are coming more and more to support research as a primary, rather than a peripheral resource, for improving education. When one compares what has been accomplished with the levels of support and commitments to research, as well as the methodology itself, to what existed fifteen years ago, the achievements must be applauded. It is only when one relates the progress made against what needs to be learned to improve education, and contrasts research investments in this field with those in other areas, such as space, health, defense, and agriculture, that past efforts and accomplishments can be assessed in proper perspective. In this type of comparison, progress toward developing a research component for education must be rated as little more than embryonic. The real birth and maturation of educational research and development as a vital force to improve learning and teaching are yet to come. Whether the movement will abort or continue to make healthy growth will depend on the united and dedicated efforts of all who are concerned with education.

The danger that progress toward developing an effective research component for education will be aborted is a real one. During the past two years, federal support for R and D in the field of education has actually declined. Some institutional centers and Regional Research Laboratories have had to be closed. Training programs have been discontinued. Of the funds available, most are committed to existing programs; very little is free to encourage new research. For example, of the $9,000,000 allocated to applied research and development, a pitifully small amount in itself, $7,000,000 go to support one project—the "Sesame Street" television program. Another $1,500,000 is allocated to other established programs, and only about $500,000 is available to underwrite new applications of research knowledge.

In comparison to federal investments in research and development in other areas, education receives only token support. Of the almost $17,000,000,000 appropriated for research and development by the Congress for the fiscal year 1972, over $8,300,000,000 went to defense; $3,200,000,000 was allocated to space research; $1,200,000,000 was appropriated for research on atomic energy; and so on—while $122,000,000 went to education. Here is another comparison. In 1971 the nation maintained a $51,500,000,000 health enterprise and is spending $2,500,000,000 on health R and D, or almost 4.7 percent of the total budget; for agriculture the year's expenditure will be $73,500,000,000 with $1,100,000,000 going to research, over 1.5 percent; while education with a $53,000,000,000 budget, will devote in all categories only $210,000,000 to research, which is less than 0.4 percent of the budget.

Creating a Constituency for Educational Research

A key reason efforts to develop a research component for education are lagging far behind progress in other fields is the absence of an effective research constituency. Too few voices are being raised in support of research in the field of education. Those that are heard are often so feeble and contradictory that they produce negative rather than positive results. The education research community, which now includes probably 10,000-12,000 members, is too insulated from the public and the rest of the education profession to rally support. Then, too, researchers generally are not trained to understand or influence the processes by which public policy is evolved to support research.[18] Leadership in schools of education in universities where educational researchers are trained and most of them employed, with a few notable exceptions, is generally insensitive to the kind of research constituency that is required and too busy with other matters to give much time to helping to develop one. Only a few state superintendents give a high priority to research in their own budgets or in their leadership to improve education. Superintendents of schools are too harassed with problems to take time to support research, and many of them actually fear that research results will only add to their burdens. Classroom teachers are not trained to use or to help conduct research; they, too, tend to fear its consequences. Professional organizations, despite the lip service some have given to research in recent years, are too busy maintaining themselves to give active leadership to creating a research constituency. Employees of the United States Office of Education cannot provide the leadership because of restrictions placed on their political activities. With all these key educational groups failing to get involved, a research constituency simply cannot exist. A few hundred volunteers, however dedicated their efforts, simply cannot mount the pressures of public and professional opinion needed to gain adequate support for educational research and development. What is needed is a working coalition of educational and citizen groups that will speak with one powerful voice in support of legislation and appropriations for educational research.[19]

The question as to who or which agency should take the lead to create a coalition of educational and citizen groups to form a viable constituency for educational research and development is a critical one. A logical answer might be the American Educational Research Association, which already has attempted to marshal and coordinate support for the legislation to create the national institute for education. The American Association of Colleges for Teacher Education, the Association of College Professors of Education, and the National Education Association itself are other possible sources of leadership. Possibly the National Academy of Education, composed as it is of a group of prestigious researchers, might be the agency to develop such a research constituency. Participating in such a coalition, if properly conceived, could relieve member organizations of the risk to their tax-exempt status. Should leadership fail to come from any existing professional or citizens' group, another possibility would be for the volunteers across the nation, who heretofore have had no formal organization, to take the lead to develop a coalition of groups into the kind of constituency needed.[20]

However a coalition constituency for educational research and development is evolved, it will need to provide for continuity of leadership and such staff help as may be required. It is important, however, not to create a large professional staff whose major concern will more likely be with maintaining the operation itself rather than working for research. Channels of communications will need to be developed to disseminate information with sufficient lead time for action. Procedures to solicit, synthesize, and unify policy recommendations of member groups and individuals will be required. In addition, it will be important to develop training programs to teach members of the coalition how research and scholarship relate to public policy, and vice versa, as well as the most effective techniques by which policy development can be influenced.[21] Another need is

to educate all to the size of the research and development component—at least 5 percent of the annual costs of education—that
will be required to supply the basic research necessary to discover
new knowledge and the extensive developmental activities essential
to translate knowledge into practice.

Important to the success of such cooperation will be the commitment of each partner to support policies that are agreed upon. If
educators work for research and development rather than against
each other, their representatives in Washington will support their
proposals. To achieve such unity, efforts will have to be directed
toward broad objectives, such as passing new legislation when needed
and achieving overall increases in research appropriations rather than
toward narrower vested-interest-type objectives. Success will depend
on the exercise by all of a high level of statesmanship that keeps the
achievement of a research and development component for education a first priority and one that is unfettered by political or professional partisanship.

*A view of the particular problems of the National Institute of Education was
given by Patricia Stivers in the* Educational Researcher.[22]

Some of the political realities involved in congressional accountability became abruptly clear to officials at the National Institute of
Education during the appropriations procedures this fall.

It has been a painful process for the institute to see a $162,000,000
budget request for fiscal 1974 get shaved to $142,000,000 by the
House, then dive to $50,000,000 during deliberations of the Senate
Appropriations Committee, and finally emerge from the Senate at
$75,000,000.

The appropriations bill has not yet completed its rounds, but if
the NIE budget remains at the $75,000,000 level, the impact will be
felt throughout the agency. In the meantime education circles are
speculating on what happened.

A serious gap in NIE's communication with the Hill was a large
part of the agency's recent difficulties, but a measure of politics was
also involved.

The going grew tough with the Senate Appropriations Subcommittee on Labor and HEW. The report of the committee criticized
NIE for "doing little to assert its role of leadership" and for "what

appears to be a total lack of understanding of purpose." The report specifically disapproved the "short shrift" given two of the career development programs transferred to NIE from the Office of Education—the Mountain-Plains Education and Economic Development program and the District of Columbia school project.

The focus on these two projects by the subcommittee is illustrative of the information gap that is central to the issue. There was keen interest in—and large financial commitments had been made to—the Mountain-Plains (Montana) and D.C., or Anacostia, projects from several corners on the Hill when the projects were still under the Office of Education. They came to NIE as veritable sacred cows. Efforts by the Career Education staff to examine cost-benefit ratios and replicability of project features were not always welcomed by local staffs. Building an R and D component into these projects to comply with NIE's primary function was "a challenge in diplomacy" according to NIE's Career Education director Corinne Rieder. The gap developed when the NIE failed to keep the Hill informed about these and other projects. Not unexpectedly, the critics were on hand to fill the gap.   ·

During the subcommittee hearings in July NIE Director Thomas Glennan faced an unfriendly—indeed hostile—Senator Warren Magnusen (D.-Wash.). He took Glennan and other witnesses to task for turning back $3,500,000 to the treasury in fiscal 1973 and for presenting only a very general definition of programs to justify a larger request. And a tactical error on Glennan's part—out-of-town commitments on the day when his reappearance before the committee was requested—did not help.

But Glennan was caught in a squeeze between the need to detail plans to the subcommittee and a provision in the authorizing legislation regarding the National Council on Educational Research. The whole matter of the council has been something of a chicken-and-egg affair. The Council is legislatively mandated to set policies of the agency before programs proceed. Theoretically, NIE should not have proceeded with its various programs until the policies for each program were established by the council. In fact, the council was not appointed by the White House until March 26, not approved until June 7, and did not meet to act officially for the first time until the first week of July.

Glennan was hit from two directions last spring for proceeding with programs in advance of council action on policies. Hearings in February by Representative John Brademas' (D.-Ind.) Select Subcommittee on Education and a March 15 lawsuit by the National Committee for Educational Change both brought pressure on the institute for operating without a council.

These developments undoubtedly contributed to the conservative approach Glennan took in describing the agency's plans in the July hearings. Early portions of the testimony carefully indicated that the budget "represents essentially staff recommendations that will be presented to Council."

During the appropriations hearings, Magnusen was persistent in questioning the turnback of $3,500,000 from fiscal 1973 funds. In defending the turnback, Glennan cited the "no-year" funds proviso of the authorizing legislation. The provision allows funds to remain available for two years to improve NIE's ability to manage discretionary research and development funds without the pressure of a frantic June 29 funding effort.

While much of the disfavor with NIE surfaced in the hearings, the agency has been the object of some lesser congressional irritations. Senator Magnusen produced the classic source of Hill displeasure— the dissatisfied constituent. He read into the record of the hearings a detailed complaint from the president of a Washington college whose research proposal had been rejected in the Field Initiated Studies review. Likewise, there were still to be counted among Washington's legislators those who did not wish to see the demise of LBJ's Office of Economic Opportunity hastened by the migration of staff to a newer agency. Some were unhappy with NIE's handling of the labs and centers.[23] And a few simply had expectations which exceeded the agency's output to date.

A more serious aspect of the problem has been a dearth of contact between NIE and legislators or their staffs on both sides of the Hill. As one House aide put it, "NIE's relationships with the Senate staff were scant. It's even been months since I've seen anyone from that agency, and I'm a friend."

Glennan's decision to rely on the HEW Hill liaison staff clearly failed to build the necessary links and supports in the Congress for NIE and its programs. Going through HEW channels instead of carrying its own message to Congress served also to create the view from the Hill that NIE was intentionally aligning itself with the administration, and that in turn left NIE very vulnerable when Nixon threatened to veto any "inflationary" HEW appropriation. The subcommittee was pressured by the White House to reduce the HEW appropriation to below the level approved by the House or face a veto. The subcommittee reaction was approximately, "If we must cut to avoid a veto, we'll cut the administration's programs."

Some criticism has been voiced of researchers for not supporting their own agency. House Education and Labor Subcommittee staff member Jack Duncan noted an imbalance between vocal critics and silent supporters from the field. "The American Federation of Teachers was actively working against the voucher program, for example, but there weren't any researchers up here speaking for the Institute," he said.

NIE supporters on the House side were clearly disappointed at the harsh reaction of the Senate committee. A more sympathetic view came during the Senate floor debate on the bill. Senator J. Glenn Beall (R.-Md.) pointed out that "NIE is only in its first year" and made a plea for a greater emphasis on research in education. He cited HEW's annual health research and development investment at "4.6% of the nation's total expenditures on health. In agriculture it is one percent of the nation's total expenditures for agriculture. But in education we are only spending three-tenths of one percent on research and development. In view of the importance of education and the size of our national efforts, current research and development seem inadequate," said Beall.

Senator Jacob Javits (R.-N.Y.) led the effort on the Senate floor to reinstate NIE's funds. In the face of heated criticism from Magnusen, Javits concentrated on giving the agency another opportunity to present its case to the conference committee. "If it's worth $75,000,000 . . . there must be something to it . . . Let them prove it," he said.

HEW Secretary Weinberger also urged the Appropriations Subcommittee to reconsider its decision. In a letter to Chairman McClellen (D.-Ark.), Weinberger expressed surprise that the subcommittee "would abruptly shift away from such a recent initiative of both Congress and the Executive—an initiative, that is just now getting underway . . . ."

But, by that time, pressures from HEW were adding to the senatorial pique. New Hampshire's Senator Norris Cotton (R.) joined the floor debate with "I'm getting jolly well fed up with having the HEW call me on the phone and tell me that I have done a horrible thing in making a cut or in approving a cut."

At this writing (mid-October 1973) the HEW appropriations bill bill has been referred to a conference committee which is in recess. The NIE portion of that budget could emerge as a compromise level between the House-approved $142,000,000 and the Senate-approved $75,000,000, but most observers are not optimistic.

If the bill is vetoed, the agencies involved would revert to a continuing resolution. That procedure normally dictates that an agency may continue to spend money at the level of the previous year's budget. But a new joint congressional provision for fiscal 1974 operations ties the amount of a continuing resolution to the lowest figure approved by either house. Or, in short, if the HEW bill is vetoed, the NIE budget for fiscal 1974 could not exceed the Senate-approved $75,000,000 level.

Glennan's reaction—"not one of overwhelming joy"—understates the atmosphere abounding at the agency facing such a possibility.

Most unfortunately for educational researchers will be the scarcity of funds for field research. According to an NIE spokesman, an early victim would be the Research Grants Program (this year's name for last year's Field Initiated Studies). Last year's program funded $11,000,000 in field research.[24] But at $75,000,000 the whole program could go. Other program areas where major cutbacks could be expected are Career Education, dissemination efforts, and many of the exploratory studies task forces where the problem-oriented research was planned in areas such as early childhood education, governance, finance, and educational personnel. Much of the research under the task forces would have been contracted out.

If the conference committee works out a compromise, and if the White House does not veto, the institute might end up with between $110,000,000 and $125,000,000, or approximately its current budget of $75,000,000 will compel NIE to make a very thorough reassessment. Indeed, $75,000,000 would be the smallest federal investment in educational R and D in more than a decade.

John Brademas was sponsor in Congress of the National Institute of Education. In a later issue of the Educational Researcher, *he presented a congressional view of the institute.*[25]

It is not to flatter the university and educational research and development communities, but because I believe it to be true, that I say those who labor to extend the frontiers of learning about learning are engaged in an enterprise crucial to the future of our society. As a member for fifteen years of that committee of the House of Representatives with chief responsibility for writing legislation for education from preschool through graduate school, I speak from experience when I say we need the best that the men and women of the educational research and development community can give us if we as legislators, and our nation as a whole, are to provide education worthy of a free people in the modern world.

It is because of this conviction that three and a half years ago I responded with such enthusiasm to President Nixon's proposal, in his message to Congress on educational reform, for the creation of a National Institute of Education as a vehicle for supporting research and development in education. Given events since that time, I think it is wise to reflect on the origins and present situation of NIE and to consider the causes of the latest developments affecting it. Then I will touch on how, as one member of Congress, I see some priorities which the institute could address. Finally, I want to make some suggestions to the professional educational research and development community for the expansion and enhancement of research and development on teaching and learning.

Creating a National Institute of Education

As one who has found it easy—and it is getting easier every day!—to restrain his enthusiasm for the works of Richard Nixon, I nonetheless applauded the president's call for establishing an institution that would, in his words, "begin the serious, systematic search for new knowledge needed to make educational opportunity truly equal." So in March 1970, as leader of a bipartisan group of twenty members of the House of Representatives, I introduced the bill authorizing the National Institute of Education.

The Select Education Subcommittee, which I have the honor to chair, of the House Committee on Education and Labor, conducted extensive hearings on the bill, visited centers of educational research in this country and abroad, and commissioned essays by leading authorities on the kinds of problems such an institute might consider.[26]

Our subcommittee went through this intensive process—a kind of protracted graduate seminar—not only to inform ourselves about the role of research in education but also to signify to our colleagues in Congress, to the administration, to educators and others that we regarded the National Institute of Education as a new development of the highest importance to the future of American education.

And, without here reviewing the legislative history, Congress wrote the National Institute of Education into law. Suggested by a Republican president not known for his support of education, approved by bipartisan majorities in a Democrat-controlled Congress, the new venture was on its way.

Difficulties of NIE

But it has become apparent that the NIE has run into some serious troubles in its first year of experience. That the $162,000,000 recommended by an antieducation administration should have been reduced to $75,000,000 by a Congress that consistently votes more money for education than the president wants is dramatic evidence of these troubles.

Why the cuts? Here, I suggest, are some reasons.

Many members of Congress are not really clear about what research in education is and, whatever it is, are not sure that research makes any difference in improving teaching and learning. Investment in research, moreover, especially in the field of human behavior, characteristically does not produce rapid, concrete dividends. The lack of short-run payoffs from educational research is all the more grating to congressmen and senators faced with an administration budget that slashes deeply or eliminates federal funds for ongoing education programs.

Another reason for the NIE's funding difficulties is, in my view, apathy or opposition from professional groups, including teachers, chief state school officers, educational organizations, and even researchers, who, not seeing some immediate benefit to their own interests, responded like some county highway commissioners complaining that there was not enough pork in the barrel for them. I must say, too, that Tom Glennan and his associates have been courageously engaged in some self-criticism on this point—that the NIE leadership should have done a much better job of communicating its purposes to Congress as well as to the educational community. The consequence is that neither congressmen charged with obligating federal funds nor teachers, school boards, state agencies, or university scholars have held aloft the standard of educational research and development as a critical enterprise in the advancement of teaching and learning.

But finally, the White House itself must bear a major share of the blame for the failure of Congress to vote more funds for NIE. By delaying for months the selection of the director and then for many months more the appointment of the National Council on Educational Research, which was deliberately designed by Congress to be policy making and not simply advisory in nature, President Nixon left the NIE leadership in a straitjacket. It was difficult for Dr. Glennan to tell Congress what his programs and policies were to be, given the absence of the council that had been statutorily mandated to share authority with the director in shaping those programs and policies.

Elsewhere I have said that I believe the mentality of Watergate is to be found throughout the administration of Richard Nixon. In my view, that mentality cropped up even in the matter of the White House attitude toward the NIE. For when I say the mentality of Watergate, I mean simply the posture of contempt for the law of the land—in this case, the willful refusal of President Nixon to obey the law which Congress wrote requiring that he appoint a National Council on Educational Research. That Mr. Nixon should have so undermined the strong bipartisan support in Congress for an initiative for which he could rightfully claim credit is a problem I leave to researchers in human behavior to explain.

Research Priorities

Before turning to what the research and development community can do to help NIE out of its difficulties, let us first examine what appear to me to be priorities for research and development in education today. I do not, of course, insist that the priorities of federal legislators are the only ones, and I recognize that mine are, understandably, colored by my particular perspective and experience. For there are other sources of priorities as well: public policy makers at all levels of government—federal, state and local; consumers—teachers, students, administrators, parents; and, of course, the practitioners of research and development, such as the members of AERA.

But here is a list of areas that, as one member of Congress, I believe should come high on the agenda of effort of NIE itself and of the institutions it engages to carry out research. As I set forth my list, I will indicate how some items relate to problems members of Congress encounter in writing education legislation.

First, we need basic research into the learning process. We should seek to understand the variety of cognitive styles that should be accommodated in the classroom. Moreover, physiologists and nutritionists should be enlisted as well as psychologists to explore factors which affect learning ability. As chief sponsor of the comprehensive child development bill, which President Nixon vetoed in 1971, I want to know—as my colleagues and I renew our efforts to shape a new early childhood proposal—all I can about how and when children learn and develop, both cognitively and noncognitively. What can researchers tell us on this matter of crucial concern?

Second, NIE should give special attention to the complex national problems of the education of the disadvantaged. The Committee on Education and Labor is currently considering legislation to extend the Elementary and Secondary Education Act. We spent many months in an effort to write Title I, which provides funds for disadvantaged students. How do you define educational disadvantage? The present law is premised on the presupposition of a very high correlation between economic deprivation and educational underachievement. And the formula I developed for distributing Title I monies, which as I write, the Committee on Education and Labor has approved, continues to rely heavily on economic deprivation as an indicator of educational disadvantage. That premise has been under attack in the committee, and none of us has seen scientific evidence that is completely compelling on any side of this argument. We need the help of the educational research community here, and most of us, frankly, have not been much impressed by what we have seen.

Third, the NIE should study educational finance at every level— from preschool through graduate school. Recent court decisions at both the state and federal levels should make us all aware that we are headed for major changes in the pattern of support of public elementary and secondary education in the United States, but it is not clear in just what direction we are going.

The sad state of our knowledge here is one of the reasons Congress established a National Commission on the Financing of Postsecondary Education as part of the Higher Education Act of 1972. We were mightily distressed by the failure of the American education community, including its researchers, to pay serious intellectual attention to the economics of higher education. Researchers might recall, for example, the several reports of recent years contending that many of our colleges and universities were in deep financial distress. But when our committee attempted to find a definition of "financial distress" or even "financial need," our inquiries fell on stony ground. For there are no commonly accepted standards of the economics of higher education, and while simply to state the problem is not to solve it, educators must realize the dangers for the future financing of higher education in the continued absence of more systematic attention to such problems by the higher education community. Or are we in Congress to be told that with respect to shaping public policy to support the institutions that symbolize reason in our society, reason does not apply?

Those of us who sat on the National Commission labored hard to fashion not a "laundry list" of legislative recommendations for Congress, but, rather, a much-needed analytical framework within which those who make decisions on financing postsecondary education—congressmen, state legislators, governors, administrators—can more soundly, more rationally, make decisions about the financing alternatives presented to them. It was not an easy task, and hopefully the National Institute of Education will find in our commission's effort to construct a framework something of value on which to build.

As a fourth priority, it seems to me that NIE should consider ways of improving the education of educators—of enhancing the qualities of those who teach in, or administer, our schools and universities. And I am concerned, in this connection, that in the headlong rush of the Nixon administration to abandon federal support for training in nearly every area, NIE not turn its back on the need for professionals trained in research and development as well as the latest teaching practices. To advance educational practice in terms of both the content of what is taught and the means by which it is taught must also be on the agenda of NIE. And it is, possibly, in these areas that the membership of the AERA has made its most significant contributions.

Fifth, I think it is essential that the National Institute have as a high priority the creation of ways of strengthening the links between research and development institutions and schools and universities. To explain why Congress gave control over dissemination to NIE rather than OE, I quote from the language of the report of our House committee on the bill establishing the National Institute of Education:

There are two reasons the Institute must collect and disseminate the findings of educational research as well as support such research. First, if they are to be aware of the needs of real students and real teachers and real administrators and real educational settings, researchers involved in developing new knowledge about learning must be involved with such consumers of education.

Second, the process of research and development in education is not a simple linear one, that is, a process in which basic research is followed by demonstration and validation and then by dissemination of a product. Rather, the process is a dynamic one in which there are constant continuing interchanges back and forth, between and among: (1) basic researchers; (2) those who demonstrate the results; and (3) the consumers, those who apply the results in teaching and learning situations.

The Institute must, therefore, assume responsibility not only for the development of educational materials and practices but also for their dissemination to students, teachers, administrators and other potential users. [27]

The Senate report on the bill echoes this view of the nature of the relationship between dissemination and research.

Sixth, beyond the existing institutions and schedules of learning, there are some emerging approaches that deserve the most searching inquiry: continuing and mid-career education, nonformal and extra-institutional ways of learning, and the relationship between the public and nonpublic sectors of education.

In this connection, should not educational researchers take heed of the implications of last spring's report of the panel of the president's Science Advisory Committee entitled "Youth: Transition to Adulthood"?

The panel, chaired by James S. Coleman, suggests, among other things, that schools, and the educators who run them, do not adequately prepare young people for adulthood and, in fact, isolate them from most useful roles in the society.

The report goes on to suggest that the objectives of schools should be expanded beyond providing students with cognitive skills to include helping young people learn to manage their own affairs, to "develop capabilities as a consumer not only of goods, but more significantly, of the cultural riches of civilization," and, finally, to develop "capabilities for engaging in intense concentrated

involvement in an activity." Will educational researchers see such
thinking as a threat or an opportunity?

I want finally to single out for special discussion as a high-priority
matter for the NIE the development of measures for assessing and
evaluating the effectiveness of education. It is wise to recall that
President Nixon, in seeking to justify the sharp reduction or elimination from his 1974 budget of federal funds for a number of
domestic programs, said, "We have conducted detailed studies comparing . . . costs and results. On the basis of that experience, I am
convinced the costs of many Federal programs can no longer be
justified." But as many of my colleagues in Congress will agree, and
as I can testify from personal experience, administration witnesses at
congressional hearings have been silent when pressed to describe the
standards and techniques by which they have judged programs successful or not. Administration witnesses have simply been unable to
point to the existence of the "detailed studies comparing . . . costs
and results" on the basis of which studies they try to justify cutbacks
in federal funds. The members of AERA know better than do most
people that we have a long way to go to develop an effective
technology of the evaluation of human behavior. A degree of
humility, therefore, would be much more in order than these
sweeping—and fundamentally dishonest—pretensions of administration spokesmen, including the president. For their pleas for budget
cutbacks in domestic programs are far more understandable in terms
of ideological bias than as a consequence of objective evaluation. So
I am very pleased to see that such groups as the National Advisory
Council on Education Professions Development are giving particular
attention in their current discussions to the problem of the
evaluation of education.[28] I believe it imperative that the NIE place
evaluation high on its list of subjects that require the most careful and
thoughtful inquiry and analysis. We need to develop a science and
technology of evaluation, and we need as well to learn how to
evaluate evaluation.

There is one paramount consideration which, in my judgment,
should underlie all the works supported by NIE, a consideration of
particular significance to AERA members. For I am sure we all can
share the conviction that a climate conducive to inquiry of the
highest quality must be established in all the work supported by the
National Institute of Education if it is to be successful in bringing
change to American education.

Future of the Institute

As we look down the road to the future of the NIE, I want to urge the researchers and developers in education in this country to give strong support to the institute. That they may not themselves have benefited from NIE as much as they hoped is really no excuse for standing by on the other side. I know that many researchers feel particularly aggrieved at a past pattern of educational R and D policy that seems at best erratic. Nevertheless, if professionals in various educational sectors are serious about the importance of research and development in education in this country, they have a responsibility to support NIE. It is the only one we have, and I believe it terribly shortsighted, as I have earlier suggested, that so many who should have a stake in supporting the efforts to improve the quality of education in this country have failed to communicate to their representatives and senators their conviction of the importance of this enterprise, or, still worse, have opposed the effort. In this connection, I want to reiterate my conviction that Tom Glennan is worthy of counsel and advice and support as well as of constructive criticism.

I hope that the members of AERA will realize that, like the rest of the country, many in Congress do not really understand the contribution that first-class research and development can make to increasing our dividends on our national investment in education. Researchers have, therefore, an educational responsibility to help the country and Congress to a better appreciation of this relationship. For on the skills, the imagination, the efforts of our educational researchers and developers depends, far more than perhaps even they realize, the capacity of American education to produce a free and civilized people.

Senator Claiborne Pell of Rhode Island gave his view of the political problems of the NIE in an address before the Council for Educational Development and Research in Washington, D.C., in 1974, an address that was later published by the Educational Researcher. [29]

The theme of your meeting, which you have invited me to discuss, is an appropriate topic. May I initially assure you, I personally believe education research to be of great importance. However, this very title assumes that there is support for education research and development in our country and, to be more specific, in the Congress. This is an assumption which I do not believe can be made.

Before we talk about "building partnerships," we must talk about the present climate or view in the Congress of education research and development. We have to talk about the existing National Institute of Education (NIE) and its future life. Right at this point, some may question why the fate of the NIE should be treated the same as that of education research and development in general. Should not it be treated as a separate governmental agency, with education research and development looked upon as a national activity? Unfortunately, to most of the members of the Senate and House, when you talk about education research, it is the NIE that comes to mind. We tend to treat it as a generic subject, and, to use a cliché, all are tarred with the same negative brush.

Unfortunately, as we are all very aware, it was unclear whether the conference on the Labor-HEW appropriations bill would bring forth any funds to continue the federal education research efforts conducted under the NIE (the Senate having recommended zero funding). Although the bill now includes $70,000,000 for NIE this precarious situation does, I believe, call for a discussion as to why we have such a problem and whether or not there is any way out.

I believe one of the major difficulties facing education research is the failure of the important education researchers in the country and the NIE to develop a so-called constituency in the Congress. The old adage that the squeaky wheel gets the grease does work on the Hill. The fact that a broad-based constituency is virtually nonexistent is evidenced by the indifference, if not hostility, in the Appropriations Committee to the funding of the NIE.

The lack of a constituency with its concomitant lack of congressional support goes back further. When the initial concept of the NIE was considered in the Education Subcommittee of the Senate, it was done as part of a compromise bill which included various ideas put forth by subcommittee members, the administration, and other senators. This is our way of creating an "agreed upon" piece of legislation. Therefore, by including the NIE, we gained the support of the administration for the Senate bill, but also included a provision which did not have the committed emotional support of a specific senator. There was, however, a strong commitment from House members who insisted upon the inclusion of an NIE in the conference on the Higher Education Amendments of 1972. Therefore, we had an agency established with support from Congress, as a compromise, and without any real senatorial constituency. This may explain the plight of the NIE today.

On the larger question of support, there is the very nature of education research and development itself. There is a very real question in the minds of people on the Hill as to the necessity for education research. Unfortunately, over the past twenty years every newspaper, national news magazine, and television show has described numerous breakthroughs and held discussions about how we will now be better equipped to teach youngsters. One week it would be a new machine; another, it was a different method of instruction. There was created a great expectation of success which would solve the nagging question of why our schools are not more successful.

Unfortunately, subsequent articles, television exposés, and discussions of test scores imply that, while children are staying in school for longer periods they appear to be learning less and less and that the caliber of education in the schools is going down and down. In the minds of Congress there dwells the question: does education research and development have any real impact on schools? Have all these new developments made any difference at all?

There is another question not adequately answered, and tied up in this problem of effectiveness is this problem of dissemination of education research so that those programs which are shown to be successful can be utilized by other education agencies. We are, therefore, talking about the generation of a demand for the product created. Under the National Institutes of Health, if a new life saving device or medical treatment is discovered, there is a strong move to adopt it in every hospital throughout the country, for it saves lives. Should research and development in the space or defense field create a new technique, there is a very strong reason to adopt it because of the cost-saving factor and the profit motivation. Such is not the case with education research and development. It is not a simple matter for a local educational agency to adopt a new method of instruction or a new type of teaching machine. Machines cost money. Teachers have to be retained. This, too, costs money. Yet, the corollary with industry and cost savings and profit does not apply. Education budgets are tight and are not prone to swift adjustments. Teachers' salaries are set years in advance, and new ideas are treated as peripheral due to the lack of available funds. In other words, there is a clear-cut lack of incentive to adopt that which has been created.

Another problem, when it comes to education and research and the Hill, is the question of communication. Educators very often speak a language of their own, one which is unintelligible to the uninitiated. It is very unrealistic for the education establishment to come to the Hill, speak arcane words and phrases, and then react in an offended manner when they are not understood. When testimony is given, it must be in simple language that generalists can comprehend, or otherwise your story will never get across.

What I have sketched out is a rather gloomy picture. However, I do not believe that I would be acting in the best interests of education research by standing here and telling you all is well. I personally believe there is need for the research you people are involved in, but I also believe we must go back to "square one" and deal with the whole question of federal involvement in education research as a new idea. We must act as if the history of the NIE has not occurred and that we are starting out with a clean slate.

You the education researchers must convince the Congress of the need for your product with a simple explanation of what you are doing, what you hope to accomplish, and how those accomplishments can be adopted by the local educational agencies.

How is this to be done? First, I caution you to consider timeliness in your research. One creates a constituency by having a product which is of interest to that constituency. Therefore, it is incumbent upon you to identify those education issues which will be before the Congress. Then we can zero in on them in the same manner that NASA did on space or NIH on cancer. This may not be intellectually agreeable to you, but it will bring your work and the congressional work together. This is not to say that other research should be set aside, but a study on a subject which the Congress has already dealt with will not create hosannas.

Concomitant with timely research is a realistic appraisal of how the research can be adopted by the local educational agency, adopted in a manner which will not generate teachers' opposition and great added expenditures. I spoke earlier of an incentive to adopt your product. This is essentially a selling job that can best be done through convincing the local school board that a desired end can be attained—that a goal can be reached which is not now being accomplished.

And, finally, the key to generating support for education research, not only on the Hill but in the country in general, is the belief that it can be successful. Theories out of a laboratory with no field experience should not be trumpeted. Real accomplishment in teaching youngsters should.

Only with this type of ammunition can people of like minds convince the Congress that there is a real federal interest and need for support of education research. We who believe in what you are doing need your help to convince our fellow members, and your help can best be given through realistic expectation and results.

Much of what I have discussed seems to be theoretic in nature, for example, the creation of a constituency, the identification of issues, and the generation of vocal support for education research throughout the country.

I submit to you that I am not speaking about general theory, for, within the next year, the Congress must consider the authorizing legislation for the NIE. The future of education research, or, I should say, the future of federal support of education research, is tied up in this congressional action.

Those of us in the Congress who believe in the necessity of education research are not the ones whom you in the field must concentrate on. But, somehow, you must bring the truths of the necessity, the efficacy, and the effectiveness of education research to those on the Hill who are of the opinion that all you need for a good school is good teachers, a blackboard, and a lot of chalk. And, until you can change that opinion, the future of the NIE (and, indeed, education research) is in doubt. You should be preparing now for that battle—and it will be a battle. I pledge you my support and aid, but I assure you that your friends on the Hill will not be successful without effective work on your part.

The point of view of a former associate commissioner for educational research was given in remarks by James Gallagher at the Annual AERA Convention in Washington, D.C., in April 1975. It also appeared in the Educational Researcher.[30]

For almost a decade I have had reason to watch, from inside and outside the bureaucracy, the reaction of the executive and legislative branches to educational research. I would like to share some of my conclusions from these observations. The comments derive from a conclusion that the reactions of key decision makers in government to educational research are basically emotional and have to be dealt with on the subjective level that is its base. Recognition of this irrationality does not relieve us of the responsibility for making a powerful logical case for educational research; it intensifies that need, but it calls for additional actions as well.

The logical and factual discussions on such matters as budget allocations in both the legislative and executive branches are merely a rational crust under which, I believe, deeper negative emotions flow about research in general, education in general, and educational research in particular. Let me briefly mention these three in order, and then discuss action alternatives available to us.

Public View of Research

Climatologists are now saying that we have reached the end of a period where the weather was uncommonly favorable for agriculture and are entering a less favorable era where the farmer is going to have to do considerable adapting. We can say the same for research in general. During the first half of this century research brought forth a cornucopia of benefits—increased crop yields, new medical discoveries, and improved business products of all kinds.

In the third quarter of this century research continued to yield many similar benefits, but, at the same time, also yielded the potential for a nuclear Armageddon, the splendid opportunity for a species-ending germ warfare, and many products that now are recognized as polluting the water we drink and the air we breathe. Is it any wonder that decision makers have some pause and ambivalence about pouring more resources into just any and all kinds of research?

Public View of Education

The public view of education has been almost unreservedly positive during the past century. While decision makers still have a basically favorable attitude toward education in general, that is now tempered by some new anger and disillusionment. The entire profession of education is held accountable for its manifest inability to do better with the economically poor and culturally different child. Representatives of the education profession promised much and, from the viewpoint of many of these governmental leaders, delivered little. However, it is the particular talent of political leaders to keep their anger under control most of the time, and not to bite people who can bite back.

So, they do not appear publicly mad at the National Education Association or other powerful organized educational groups. Not many leaders in executive or legislative branches hanker to take on the AFL-CIO, but they have few worries about retaliation if they take on educational research which displays the major requisites of a good scapegoat. It is visible, there are reasons to be mad at it, and it cannot effectively strike back.

Public View of Educational Research

Many decision makers see educational researchers as the intellectuals, the eggheads of the education profession; a group of rear-echelon soldiers enjoying their privileges but providing little help for the front-line troops, the teachers.

It can well and truly be argued that such a portrait is unfair: educational research, we can explain, is still in its professional infancy and yet has been asked questions that would baffle other professions who have a much richer and longer scientific past upon which to draw. Such explanations are shrugged off by many of these leaders as irrelevant excuses. They point out that when money was available for research into the disadvantaged child, they did not hear too many disclaimers about the immaturities or inadequacies of the profession.

The problem for educational research has been compounded by the fact that the most publicized findings have been unpleasant for decision makers. One can take the Coleman Report as a splendid example of educational research that causes problems for decision makers. This report, the results of which were widely circulated in Washington, forced many of these leaders into supporting desegregation and busing when they would rather not have had to face such controversial policy issues.

When educational researchers discover that school problems often reflect characteristics of the total cultural environment, it means that decision makers must accept the responsibility to make major changes in social institutions and social mores, if the social problems are to be solved. Few leaders will thank the person bringing that message. The modification of our social structure cannot be done without great pain and sorrow to all involved, particularly the leaders. With the multitude of other problems facing them, it is psychologically understandable that decision makers have limited enthusiasm for supporting an enterprise like educational research that frequently has brought such news.

All of this does not mean that educational researchers should shade the truth or try to tell the policy makers what they want to hear. If we did that, we would truly destroy ourselves. What it does mean is that we should not expect a kiss on the forehead when the news we *must* report is not always to the liking of the recipient.

Action Alternatives

If this portrait of decision makers' attitudes is basically accurate, then there is a less favorable climate for the support of educational research than we would wish. If we wish to adapt to the climate, to nurture our logically compelling arguments for increased resources, it seems to me we have several alternatives. Each alternative has a large cost attached, which makes it hard for us to buy any of them enthusiastically.

One clear choice open to us would be to attempt to obtain a more effective alliance between the educational researcher and those politically powerful education consumer groups who represent the teacher, administrator, citizen, and parent. The cost of such an alignment is obvious. We would have to pay a great deal more attention to consumer needs and requests than we have done in the past. We cannot operate in an isolated or independent fashion and expect much consumer support. A new emphasis on development which synthesizes and translates research into usable consumer products would be one way to convince other educators that the research enterprise is interested in, or wants to help, in the problems they have. Consumers want help and just will not wait the required time for new research to be completed and transformed into usable products and procedures.

Another alternative would be to find an organizational tent for shelter in inclement weather. Such shelter could be obtained by placing research in education under the administration of educational service programs themselves. The budgets of research efforts in vocational education and education of the handicapped have done well in recent years. This is not because research in these fields has been more valued, but because decision makers value the total program effort in the vocational and handicapped fields, and if the educational leaders want to include research in a total program, the decision makers do not object.

A third strategy would be to attempt to turn around public opinion with a type of startling breakthrough in some fashion similar to the Manhattan Project. This would mean major involvement by important sectors of the profession in achieving a visible, socially desirable, politically important goal.

Problem areas such as early developmental delay, reading, behavior problems, educating the handicapped, and delinquency might yield significantly to a coordinated national effort, but there seems little likelihood that such an enterprise would be acceptable to many professionals who have a hard time working with even one other colleague, and who prefer solitude to group decision making.

A fourth alternative is the status quo. This is as much of a decision as any other and carries its costs just like the other possibilities. There seems little likelihood that the National Institute of Education, with few true friends in the executive branch or Congress, will be able to mount the effort that is needed to break out of the Catch 22 situation it now finds itself in. That is, it will not get more funds until it proves what it can do, and it cannot prove what it can do without more funds.

The clear message to me is that we must either turn around the image that these key decision makers have of us with significant and visible professional action toward significant and visible accomplishments and/or we must form alliances with powerful organizations that will give us the time to prove what we are capable of doing. Power can be a temporary substitute for a mature professional, scientific and technical competence, which always takes time to achieve.

I hope that the American Educational Research Association will devote some of its considerable professional resources to addressing, through organizational initiatives, both the full delineation of the policy problems touched on here and the exploration of alternative

strategies to allow us to escape this educational Catch 22. It is clear
that a few well-chosen words offered once a year at the AERA
meetings will not change or improve anything.

*In response to these and other similar statements, the Council of the American
Educational Research Association approved the establishment of a professional
liaison program within the association charged with the responsibility of "building communication linkages and improving understanding between educational
researchers and policy makers, providing a knowledge resource to Congress, and
promoting collaborative and supportive efforts within the educational community." This is a new policy for the association, which in the past has been
almost solely concerned with communications among researchers, particularly
furnishing a forum for reporting, discussing, and criticizing research projects
and activities. In an editorial in* Educational Researcher, *William J. Russell,
executive officer of the American Educational Research Association, described
the new program:* [31]

The program AERA proposes to undertake will include a number
of activities. A two-way educational process that informs legislators
and key congressional staff about the nature of educational research
and educational researchers about the nature of the legislative process
is central to the program. It is too little, too late to write complaining to the legislator after the program has been developed, the bill
passed, and the regulations put into force. A proactive effort is
needed where previously educational researchers have only reacted to
the crisis. The legislature needs to be kept informed in the legislative
development stage of the needs of a field and the impact of a proposed bill.

A communications effort about educational research, what it is
and what it is not, what it can do and what it cannot, will be directed
at other branches of the broad education community. The effort
will include steps to improve the dialogue between educational
researchers and educational practitioners—administrators, teachers,
and other professionals whose decisions could be better informed if
the educational research field made greater efforts to demonstrate
how results can be utilized. This effort will involve working with
other professional associations and developing articles and publications which discuss research in comprehensible language. Key researchers and association governing bodies and committees will be
encouraged to speak out on major and controversial issues to enhance
the effort to make the researcher's views generally known.

Similarly, greater initiative will be taken to develop liaisons with working education reporters whose now infrequent columns on in-depth subjects where research has had an impact could help to better inform the general public of the role of research. The emergence of privacy regulations regarding school records, as a current specific example,[32] demands an effort to make parents and administrators understand, for example, the need to retain records for long-range studies.

The program is concerned with the spectrum of interest of the educational research community and not with the special interests of any one segment or subject area. It will be supported in large part by contributions from nonprofit educational R and D institutions and universities who have been asked to affiliate with the association in support of the effort. Individuals wishing to strengthen the effort will also have the opportunity to offer small contributions, however, there will be no increase in dues to support the program . . . .

The text of the statement presented by the AERA to congressional committees on the reauthorization of the National Institute of Education read as follows:[33]

The American Educational Research Association expresses its support of the National Institute of Education and the extension of its authorization beyond the fiscal 1975 period. The institute, with its new leadership, can play an important role in improving educational research, development, dissemination, evaluation, and the assessment of educational needs. These activities should always be planned in consultation with citizens and educators at all levels, both researchers and practitioner-consumers.

We support the continuation of the council and the several changes in provisions concerning membership on the council and quorum requirements as helpful in providing continuity of policy direction given to the institute staff and to HEW.

We support the research fellowship provision which will make possible more extensive consultation and communication between field researchers and the staff of the institute.

We support the efforts to provide a greater focus for educational research by identifying five priority areas, while expressing concern that other major areas for research—including education and the arts, citizenship education, violence in the schools, as examples—be preserved as options at the discretion of the council and staff. The institute should always be alert to identifying and supporting new topics for timely and productive research.

An original objective for the institute, that of research on teachers' effectiveness, should be included on the permanent research agenda, since so much formal instruction takes place in the classroom, and this topic should be highlighted as a vital component of educational productivity.

This association supports the continuation of two other features of the legislation: the provision of staff appointments excepted from civil service requirements, and the requirement that 90 percent of institute's research budget be spent on research in the field through grants and contracts. These features allow the institute to call upon the best of available talents throughout the field of educational R and D.

AERA expresses concern about two features of the authorization bill, H.R. 5988, and suggests these modifications:

The period of authorization should be extended from three to at least five years fiscal 1976 - fiscal 1980.

Greater financial support should be authorized, with planned increases in the institute's budget of $35,000,000-$50,000,000 for each of the five years.

Only through this kind of increased dollar investment and long-term legislative commitment and stability in the life of the institute can research hope to find ways to stimulate enough study on the critical issues outlined and attack such complicated problems as equal opportunity, productivity, career preparation, and effective dissemination of research findings to teachers and agencies who use the results to make a difference in the nation's classrooms.

This review of experience, opinions, and responsive actions indicates that the outlook for substantial federal support for educational research and development is a contingent one. The federal government is not likely to furnish large increases in funds for educational R and D programs like those of the past fifteen years. In fact, the Congress and the public seem disappointed and disillusioned about the value of research in improving educational effectiveness. Thus, reductions in appropriations rather than increases can be expected unless there are marked changes in the situation. Some of the possible changes are suggested in this chapter. Others are presented in subsequent ones.

Notes

1. Sidney P. Marland, Jr., "A New Order of Educational Research and Development," *Phi Delta Kappan* 52 (June 1971): 576-578.

2. Lindley J. Stiles, "Developing a Research Component for Education," *Journal of Educational Research* 65 (January 1972): 197-203.

3. Included in the group were: Dr. Francis Chase, University of Chicago; Dr. Laurence D. Haskew, University of Texas; Dr. Paul Jacobson, University of Oregon; Dr. Francis Keppel, Harvard University; Dr. Willard Olson, University of Michigan; Dr. I. James Quillen, Stanford University; Dr. Felix Robb, George Peabody College for Teachers; and myself.

4. I am indebted to both the University of Wisconsin and to Northwestern University for permitting me to devote time and energy to such efforts while in their employment. During the years 1962-1966, Dr. Joseph Totaro shared with me responsibility for this work.

5. I have had at times over 800 names on the mailing list. The names of inactive persons are dropped periodically to reduce time and costs. There have never been any form of organization, any constitution bylaws, any officers, any dues. We have been held together by a common commitment to work to develop a research component for education.

6. At that time few professional publications included information about educational research legislation and appropriations. Those that did reached readers after it was too late to influence decisions.

7. When the first team of witnesses for educational research and development appeared in 1960 before the Subcommittee of the House Education and Labor Committee, Chairman John Fogarty complimented the group for making what he called, "the best case for educational research the Congress has ever heard." Then [he] added, "Where the hell have you been up to now?"

8. Dr. Richard Dershimer, executive officer for the AERA, and individual officers and members had worked for research legislation and appropriations over the years. The action in 1969 made it possible for Dr. Dershimer to organize actively membership support and to make full use of publications of the association to disseminate information about the proposed National Institute of Education.

9. We have learned that each president of the United States likes to "put his brand" on important social service ventures. President Kennedy promised during his campaign to establish the research center program. The statement he made was written by one of the volunteers. Lyndon Johnson carried out the Kennedy pledge and then after winning reelection established as his contribution to educational research the Regional Research Laboratories. President Nixon, who never got around to making a statement prepared for him by a volunteer during his campaign against John F. Kennedy—which may explain why he lost that election—proposed the idea of a national institute for education. Our strategy has been to encourage each candidate for the presidency to promise to do something special for educational research.

10. A letter in my files from the late Senator Robert F. Kennedy expresses

appreciation of testimony presented before the Senate subcommittee which turned the tide of opinion in favor of the Elementary and Secondary Education Act legislation.

11. Another commissioner of education who worked for educational research and development was Dr. Sterling McMurrin. Although in office only a short while, he helped promote research appropriations and since leaving that post has made valuable contributions to building support for education R and D through his work with the Committee for Economic Development. See the report of the Research and Policy Committee of the Committee for Economic Development, *Innovation in Education: New Directions for the American School,* published by the Committee for Economic Development in July 1968.

12. See the interview with Congresswoman Edith Green, "U.S. Representative Edith Green: The Business of Education," *Nation's Schools* 86 (December 1970): 40-45. It is significant that she supported legislation in the subcommittee of the House in October 1971 after learning from volunteers back home that they wanted her to do so.

13. Committee for Scientific and Technical Personnel Reviews of National Educational Policies, *Educational Research and Development in the United States* (Washington, D.C.: U.S. Department of Health, Education, and Welfare, 1969), 275.

14. U.S. Office of Education, *Educational Research and Development: Its Impact and Promise* (Washington, D.C.: U.S. Department of Health, Education, and Welfare, 1970).

15. Excluding special programs, the appropriation for educational research and development for fiscal 1972 was only $122,000,000.

16. U.S. Office of Education, *Educational Research and Development in the United States* (Washington, D.C.: U.S. Department of Health, Education, and Welfare, 1970); *id., Educational Research and Development: Its Impact and Promise;* Organization of Economic Cooperation and Development, *Educational Research and Development in the United States* (Paris: the Organization, 1969).

17. *Research for Tomorrow's Schools,* ed. Lee Cronbach and Patrick Suppes (New York: Macmillan, 1969); J. H. McGrath, *Research Methods and Designs for Education* (Scranton, Pa.: International Textbook Co., 1970).

18. Dr. Ralph Tyler is a notable exception who has walked the halls of Congress to solicit support for educational research and development. There are others, too numerous to mention but too few to achieve the impact needed.

19. An example of this type of coalition is found in the field of health. Eight organizations have joined to promote appropriations for the National Institutes of Health, the Federal Health Services, and the Mental Health Administration. A characteristic of this coalition is the boldness with which it presses for funds. For 1972 the coalition asked for $5,500,000,000, which was $2,200,000,000 more than the administration had proposed.

20. All interested in achieving a research and development component for education, and particularly anyone working to form coalitions of support, will find instruction in what has been done in the pure science. See Daniel S. Greenberg, *The Politics of Pure Science* (New York: World Publishing Co., 1967).

21. Above all, the coalition should promote individual rather than bloc actions. Congressmen discount communications that are known to come from organized pressure groups. One reason the volunteers have been effective is that each has spoken only for himself, in his own way, of an interest in improving education in his state. The function of the coalition should be to promote wider involvement, more effective communications, and the coordination of ideas— rather than uninformed vested pressures.

22. Patricia Stivers, "NIE: Learning about Congress the Hard Way," *Educational Researcher* 2 (November 1973): 8-9.

23. James Welsh, "Labs and Centers: Cold Winds from Washington," *ibid.*, 1 (December 1972): 14.

24. James Welsh, "FIS Awards: Funds for One in Fifteen," *ibid.*, 2 (August 1973): 8-9.

25. John Brademas, "A Congressional View of Education R & D and NIE," *ibid.*, 3 (March 1974): 12-15.

26. The subcommittee hearings and other publications are still a valuable compendium of views on education R and D. "To Establish a National Institute of Education," Hearings before the Select Subcommittee, 92nd Congress, 1st Session (February-June 1971). Appendices: "Educational Research: Prospects and Priorities"; "Purpose and Process: Readings in Educational Research and Development"; "Alternative Futures in American Education"; "Educational Research in Europe: Report of the Select Subcommittee on Education" (December 1971).

27. House of Representatives, 92nd Congress, 1st Session, Report No. 92-554, October 8, 1971, 65-66.

28. The council has a major report in preparation, but has issued a preliminary statement, "Evaluation of Education: In Need of Examination," available from the council, 1111 20th St., N.W., Suite 308, Washington, D.C. 20036.

29. Claiborne Pell, "Building Partnerships for Educational Research and Development," *Educational Researcher* 4 (January 1975): 11-12.

30. James J. Gallagher, "The Prospects for Governmental Support of Educational Research," *ibid.* (July-August 1975): 13-14.

31. William J. Russell, "AERA's Professional Liaison Program: A New Thrust," *ibid.* (February 1975): 3-4.

32. Carolyn B. Davis, "The Buckley Regulations: Rights and Restraints," *ibid.*, 11-13.

33. "On the Record: Support for NIE," *ibid.* (July-August 1975): 1.

4. SOME MISTAKES
AND SHORTCOMINGS

In the recent rapid expansion of financial support for programs of educational research and development some errors were made, and some shortcomings were revealed. Among these weaknesses, five kinds appear to be most serious: limited competence of some investigators; unethical behavior of some investigators and research directors; lack of competent management both in the research institution and in the agency furnishing funds; lack of adequate background and competence of some contract officers; and lack of mature systems for effective management of research and development activities. These are not inherent weaknesses, but are limitations that can be overcome. But the future of educational research and development is strongly influenced by the extent of these difficulties and the rate at which they can be surmounted.

The limited competence of many researchers is not confined to the field of educational research. In 1968 a review of 200 completed research projects supported by the National Science Foundation revealed that less than 15 percent of them had produced any new knowledge. When one considers the fact that all initial proposals for projects supported by the NSF have been examined and recommended by panels of the researchers' peers, it seems probable that these projects are better than many others that are being carried on in colleges and universities. A fair conclusion is that many who would like to engage in research are not sufficiently competent to bring it off, just as many who would like to write the great novel are unable to do so. A wiser investment of research funds can be made by concentrating much more heavily upon the work of those who are highly competent.

Some of this effort to conduct research on the part of those with limited competence and often without real intellectual curiosity is due to the notion that all university professors should be researchers. For more than 250 years after the founding of the first American college, professors did not consider research as one of their accepted functions. The Ph.D. program of German universities attracted American scholars to study in Germany during the latter half of the nineteenth century. Between 1880 and 1895 three universities were founded that gave major emphasis to research—Clark University, Johns Hopkins University, and the University of Chicago. After World War I graduate programs in research became increasingly popular, and faculties produced a continuous flow of research studies. That flow has probably reached its peak of prestige. While the popularity of research among professors was growing, a folklore developed alleging that there is no inherent conflict between teaching and research. On the contrary, it was felt that an active researcher is a better teacher than one not engaged in research and that research is usually carried on with the aid of students who learn in the process of their work. It is also claimed that good faculty members can be attracted to colleges and universities only if there are excellent opportunities for them to carry on research.

No valid evidence has been submitted, nor has any been obtained, to support these views. The claims fail to recognize the different and special conditions required for effective teaching and productive research. Each of these functions requires intelligent effort and concentration of time and energy in appropriate settings. In contrast, the present dominant view holds that teaching requires only competent scholars to present to students some of the things they know and that research requires only time, facilities, and assistants to be provided every college professor. The result is ineffectiveness in both respects. More students are poorly guided in their learning efforts, and relatively few faculty members contribute significantly to the formulation of knowledge. Policies and practices need to be greatly modified in order to improve the quality of both educational research and teaching.

The situation is different with regard to competence in educational development. Heretofore the understanding of development problems and the skills required has been largely divided between authors in schools and colleges and the personnel of publishing companies. Initial efforts of professors to carry on the full range of development activities have demonstrated a lack of competence at several key points. They have not assessed the demands of society and the needs of students in order to formulate important objectives. They have not been skillful in translating needs into appropriate objectives for learning by students. They have not utilized systematic surveys of teachers' needs. They have not been markedly skillful in the design of instructional systems and materials. These things can be learned, and a few centers, like the University of Pittsburgh and Carnegie-Mellon University, offer programs of training in some of these skills, but it is not clear whether future development will largely be centered in nonprofit organizations or commercial publishers.

Edith Green, congresswoman from Oregon and an influential member of the Committee on Education and Labor of the House of Representatives, attacked severely both the management competence of those responsible for educational research and development projects and the ethical practices of some researchers. Her article is reprinted here because it presents these shortcomings clearly and forcefully.

Mrs. Green has raised two very critical questions relating to the prospect for educational research and development in the future. Can the educational research community develop and provide strong enough sanctions for a code of ethics that protects the public from greed and other unethical urges of some researchers? Can the federal government and the organizations that conduct research develop the competence in management required for the expanded programs now in operation?[1]

During the past decade, the federal government has made many new attempts to aid in the solution of the country's major problems. Great hopes and high ideals underlay these attempts. For the most part, the motives of those who championed new programs were good, and the people supporting these programs were truly representative of a national will to do something about many of the larger problems that plague our times.

As plans turned to realities, in attempting to provide solutions to our country's pressing ills, we have set up a monstrous apparatus that can no longer be supervised or controlled by even the best of men. This tremendous proliferation of programs and activities is leading to a major collapse of rational management. We are becoming ever more aware of the pitfalls we were warned about by former President Lyndon Johnson, when he said that "Legislation should not be examined in the light of benefits it will convey if properly administered— but by wrongs it would cause if improperly administered."

What is true of government in general is true as well of the federal presence in education. The Office of Education will supervise the expenditure of over $5,000,000,000 in fiscal 1972, through programs that take over seven printed pages to list. Other federal agencies and departments will pour additional billions from federal coffers into educational enterprises. The duplication, complexity, and sheer weight of these efforts are becoming unbearable to taxpayers and officials alike. Thus, the first major problem we have to face today is how to restore a rational form to our government, and keep it in a manageable form.

Closely related to this problem is a second one, namely, the extent to which education is becoming allied with business and industry. It might be useful to place this problem in the perspective of history. Educators have always wanted to have a decent income; in this respect, they have never been different from the rest of humanity. But it has been customary to realize that financial benefits were simply means to greater ends, and the ends were clear: the pursuit of knowledge, the discovery of truth, and the transmission of our cultural heritage.

Only recently have the means become ends in themselves. It is a very modern phenomenon to find educators busily at work accumulating wealth as an academic pursuit in its own right. We have entered the era of the large-scale education industry, complete with all the excesses that so often appear in a burgeoning big business.

It is sad to say that a well-meaning governmental policy has probably been largely responsible for this development. During the past decade, Congress has supported education more generously and vigorously than ever before. Very large sums of money, funding innumerable new programs, have been made available at every level of the educational ladder, from preschool to postdoctoral. Whether the result has been an improvement in education is not entirely clear; only time will tell, and only serious evaluations will help us find out. But one thing *has* become evident: the result of all this federal funding has been, directly and indirectly, the personal enrichment of some, and the runaway growth of a great many educational institutions and private corporations.

For several years now I have been particularly interested in what I have come to call the "education-poverty-industrial complex"—people and companies devoted to reaping profit from the nation's legitimate interest in education and welfare. What I have learned has not been encouraging. Studies made at my request by my staff and by the General Accounting Office have revealed serious irregularities in numerous areas. Over and over again, we have found educators enriching themselves at public expense through sizable consulting fees, often for work of which there is no record at all. Over and over again, we have found educational organizations taking money for work not done, for studies not performed, for analyses not prepared,

for results not produced. Over and over again, we have found educators using public funds for research projects that have turned out
to be esoteric, irrelevant, and often not even research.

Perhaps the precise nature of the problems we face today will be
illuminated by a specific example of a case study from my office
files. The example I have chosen is neither the best nor the worst of
those studied to date; rather, it is quite average in many respects, and
for this reason it serves quite well to help underline the deep systemic
problems, not the unusual and extraordinary failures.

The case study outlined in the next section represents a total
governmental outlay of some $60,000. This may seem a trivial
amount by comparison with the billions spent by the Office of
Education, but in fact contracts of this size are typical of OE's
operation. Consider the projects being funded by OE's National
Center for Educational Research and Development (NCERD, formerly
the Bureau of Research) in 1970. There was a total of 1,151 projects,
as recorded in NCERD's massive directory for July 1970. This total
broke down as follows: 368 projects in the under $10,000 range;
404 projects in the $10,000-$100,000 range; 318 projects in the
$100,000-$1,000,000 range; and 61 projects in the over $1,000,000
range. From this it can be seen that a contract in the amount of
$60,000 typifies a category of OE activity that is representative of
OE-funded projects—a category that is, when added up, quite significant fiscally in the overall picture.

Although the names of all parties concerned in the case have been
protected, all the details of the following story are true, and are
based on data preserved in the NCERD files.

A Case in Point

In the spring of 1968, what appears to have been an unsolicited
project proposal was received by OE. It was submitted by Professor
A. of New York through S.R., a private firm based in Washington,
where the work was to be done. The idea was to study in a thorough
and extensive manner the sociological aspects of one particular facet
of higher education policy. The project was to extend from July
1968 to September 1969.

The basic point of the proposed study is explained in the opening
paragraph of the proposal. Immediately thereafter, the basic weakness of the proposal is candidly exposed—to wit, the absence of a

concrete plan: "We would like to stress at this point that many of the details of the following outline are necessarily tentative. They illustrate what we are after and the ways we shall proceed; many additional details, though, will have to be developed and others revised as our study progresses." The proposal contains no background information at all, no context, no reference to other work, no methodology or plan, no curriculum vitae of the principal investigator (or anyone else).

At the end, A. writes: "Our ultimate purpose is to provide information and analysis to serve the needs of policy-makers . . .

Products:

1. A report . . . including background data and reasons for conclusions reached.

2. The training of a sociologist in educational research . . . ." The aim is to give the government advice, via a report. The exact meaning of product number two, "The training of a sociologist in educational research," is nowhere explained or even referred to in the body of the proposal.

The total funds requested for the study come to about $70,000. (All figures are approximate.) Of this, $21,000 is for overhead, $3,000 for a fee. Salaries and benefits are to total $42,000, according to the following breakdown of effort: half time for the director (at a rate of $30,000 per year for full time) and half time for a research associate (at a rate of $17,000 per year for full time) for the period September 1968-September 1969, and consultant status for these two (*sic!*) for July and August 1968; half time for a secretary; full time for a junior research assistant. A., the director, is the only person identified by name.

The first reaction to this proposal must be one of puzzlement. There is a lot of broadly descriptive (and fairly simpleminded and obvious) material, but virtually no specifics; yet there is quite a price tag. What is it all about?

The first reaction on file came from B.N. of OE, in a hastily written memorandum to D.O. It reads in full: "B. and P. feel that the A. proposal is too expensive and see it in the $40-$50,000 range and not $70,000. Will you look it over to see how we can pare it down." B. and P. are OE officials. They clearly have no problem at all with the product being bought, just a bit of a complaint about the price.

On that day, requests for evaluation were sent to two outside readers. The evaluations were returned within a few days. One recommended flat disapproval. The summary stated the case plainly:

I do not feel that this is a good study; nor is it a good proposal. Reason: The proposal does not specify the methodology, other than a broad and unbounded discussion of the several levels that may be influenced by a specific type of policy to assist higher education . . . . At best it is wordy, not focused, unspecific, and carries no measure of effectiveness as to how policy makers may choose. I can not approve a research proposal on the basis of hope . . . . I am not sure that the author is fully acquainted with the world of education . . . .

Under "Educational Significance," the evaluator writes "Negative" and goes on to complain that "the proposal does not suggest any real familiarity with educational literature or recent experience with ESEA or HEA." The comment on "Personnel and Facilities" reads: "No resume of personnel resources was attached. I have no way of knowing if the author is capable except on the basis of the proposal—which is very weak." He finds the research design "very poor," and the economic efficiency "extremely poor."

The second evaluation came back with a recommendation for provisional approval. The summary is not too encouraging:

The applicant has identified an area of great importance to the future of American higher education, and is a highly creative investigator who can be expected to generate valuable insights. However, there are several areas of vagueness in the proposal—possibly due to necessary shortness of time in its preparation—which ought to be remedied before a formal award is made. I would propose the following modifications to be negotiated:
    1. The applicant should satisfy the OE staff of his knowledge of existing materials in the area of inquiry . . . .
    2. The caliber of the "Research Associate" should be specified to the satisfaction of the USOE staff. (Note, on p. 11, that one "product" is to be the "training of a sociologist in educational research." At a salary of $17,000/yr., one would expect to hire someone who was *already* well trained!)
    3. The "Fee" . . . should be eliminated from the budget or justified to the satisfaction of OE staff . . . .

The evaluator goes on to note that "the work envisioned here parallels recent developments within the Bureau of the Budget and the planning offices of the several federal agencies." He finds the proposal "very vague on methodology." He is concerned that "duplication of effort is to be avoided," and notes that the proposal is silent on this question, since "the applicant fails to relate his proposed study to similar work, in any *explicit* manner." And again, he comments that the research design is "the weakest part of the proposal," and that "the budget total strikes me as somewhat high."

In light of all these criticisms, how could he recommend provisional approval? The answer lies in his comments under "Personnel and Facilities." So great is the evaluator's regard for A. that this outweighs his concern about the rest of the background support:

A. is an outstanding sociologist, highly imaginative, and a prolific worker. There should be some specification of the qualifications of the proposed Research Associate. The S.R. probably lacks library resources which would be required to relate the proposed work to relevant literature in the field. I would *hope* that creative computer people would be available within the S.R., to experiment with system simulation, but this hope isn't directly justified by the contents of the proposal.

In mid-June, D.O. provided his opinion of the proposal, in an "in-house review." As we learn from the various official forms, D.O. had been designated project officer for this study. On the question of educational significance, he had this to say: "The problem of policies for federal support of higher education is of top priority (see President's Education Message); but I am not sure how much hard data this project would furnish on the problem as distinguished from intuitive and informed guesses." He notes candidly that there are "no clear research design . . . no hypothesis, no experimental procedures, no reference to related research, no procedures described." Also, he writes, under "Economic Efficiency": "Cost higher than necessary. Do we need to train a sociologist in educational research at $17,000 a year? The 'fee' . . . is unjustified when indirect costs . . . are incurred." But despite these faults, he recommended approval. His reasoning is presented at the outset of the review: "This is not really a research proposal but a proposal to engage the services of a competent and inventive sociologist to forecast the 'futures' of American higher education and patterns of federal support. It should be coordinated with the Secretary's task force on strategies of support (e.g., Bob Berk) and Clark Kerr's Commission on the Future of Higher Education." And again, later: "This is a proposal essentially to fund a well-known sociologist to think about higher education."

The sequence of events leading to the actual contract award bordered on comic opera. The Funding Approval Request originated by D.O. in mid-June—just two weeks before the end of the fiscal year deadline—obtained its final signature within a week; it called for fiscal year 1968 funding in the total of $45,000 for this project. Where did the figure $45,000 come from? We shall never know. It certainly is not the amount requested by A., and there is no other document presenting a budget in that amount. The only plausible explanation relates to the memo of B.N. quoted above, calling for something "in the $40-$50,000 range"—$45,000 being right in the middle of the range. At any rate, for the time being, $45,000 was the magic figure. The Procurement Action Request executed in the last week of June also carried that figure, as did D.O.'s Schedule of Negotiable Items, which was entirely blank except for the total project cost, listed as $45,000, without any indication of how OE wanted S.R. to cut their proposal to that figure.

Apparently, despite all the effort, fiscal 1968 was missed, so the procedure had to start all over again in July. A new Procurement Action Request was issued in early July, calling again for $45,000, but this time in fiscal 1969 funds. Meanwhile, mid-July saw some negotiations between OE and S.R. We have some handwritten memos from that period discussing several issues, among which were the following: (1) the size of S.R.'s overhead rate; (2) the propriety of a fee (which, in the end, S.R. received); (3) the propriety of hiring a $17,000-a-year man for "training," an objection raised, as we saw, during the evaluations; (4) the propriety of paying the director in a consultant status during the summer; and (5) the "need for clerk and sec'y for 1 person."

Whatever the mechanism that finally did the trick, S.R. got the message, and produced a slightly reduced budget—a "revised cost estimate"—at the end of July. The covering letter explains that two reductions were involved: (1) the provisional overhead rate was dropped to 50 percent; (2) the junior research assistant's time was cut back drastically, from full time for the whole fifteen months, to approximately one-fourth time. In this way, the budget was brought down to $55,000. Actually, the first reduction was a pure fiction, because a final overhead rate was to be established later, quite apart from the provisional rate, and the government would end up paying in full whatever the final overhead rate would turn out to be.

The end of July thus saw a $10,000 discrepancy between the $45,000 asked for OE's Procurement Action Request and the revision downward to $55,000 offered by S.R. What was OE to do? It apparently never occurred to anybody to say to S.R., "Take the $45,000 or leave it." Instead, with no justification, the $10,000 was added, with the aid of subterfuge. D.O. sent a memo to the chief of the Contracts Division asking for the additional funds, with the following explanation: "Reason for the increase over amount authorized in original Procurement Action Request is that the overhead rate was inadvertently left out in the proposed budget when [NCERD] approved the proposal." The absurdity of this explanation could have been revealed at a glance, since the sum requested had no relation at all to any overhead shown on any version of the proposal.

But no matter; it was an unimportant detail. A new request for the additional amount went out, and by the beginning of September, a contract was ready. Five days later, A. wrote OE the happy news that he was now in Washington at S.R., although the letter had to be signed by someone else "in Dr. A.'s absence"!

A disturbing note disrupts the peaceful progress of A.'s cogitation at OE expense. In September, one Dr. J.B. wrote OE asking for help and information regarding a study he had begun *with OE funds* on the same subject! There was obviously considerable overlap with A.'s work, although not one person involved with either project—in or out of OE—knew that the other was taking place! When the two projects had been funded, no one had checked to see whether there might be others doing the same thing! D.O.'s reply asked J.B. for a copy of his proposal and the names of his OE project officers. Apparently D.O. knew that he could get the information from J.B. more rapidly than he could extract it from the OE bureaucracy of which he himself was a part.

Such duplication, unfortunately, is far from unusual. Part of the problem is OE's abysmal records system, which is virtually useless. Thus, it is almost impossible to obtain accurate information—or even sketchy information, for that matter—on such questions as what projects are currently being funded, what projects have recently been completed, what contractors or grantees hold which contracts or grants, and so forth. Part of the problem is OE's incredibly complex—and ever-changing!—internal organization, which allows for numerous overlaps in authority and which seems to encourage random duplication in various fields.

To return to our narrative: The first progress report was submitted around the beginning of the new year and was quickly accepted by D.O. The report covered the first four months of work, about one-third the total length of the project. The first paragraph told it all: "In line with our study design the first period of our research has largely involved (1) a preliminary survey of the literature, especially works which attempt to give an overall view of the higher education system, (2) acquaintance with the data base, and (3) refinement of the research design." The word "preliminary" in (1) really meant just that, as we are told that "in the months that have elapsed . . . we have only been able to cover a small fraction of the literature on higher education . . . . We are increasingly focusing on literature that reports specific empirical findings relevant to our problem."

Thus, very little had been accomplished, and most of the time had been spent in highly eclectic reading. What the staff was doing was not clear. Since there had been no research design in the first place, no one at OE could complain. But by the time a few months had passed, it had already become clear that A. was not necessarily a good choice even as a consultant, since he was barely acquainted with the field—something that the proposal evaluators had warned about. It appears that the sociologist who was being "trained" in education research was A. himself!

The end of March 1969 brought the second progress report; the halfway point had already been reached. The three-page report repeatedly stressed how complex the problems are. The first paragraph again tells the essential story of what was going on:

Since the last progress report we have focused primarily on two tasks:
(1) A relatively detailed survey of the current programs of federal assistance to higher education and the proposals for additional assistance, and the development of conceptual tools to facilitate their analysis.
(2) Determining the probable consequences of "ideal-type" forms of aid for educational opportunity, and more generally social stratification.

It must have heartened OE personnel to learn that A. was at last becoming acquainted with the existing federal programs. But we do not find out very much about the kinds of "conceptual tools" that were being developed, or the "probable consequences" that were being looked at.

This report was so loose and chatty that it obviously got on D.O.'s nerves. By the end of April he had worked up the determination to do something; not, of course, anything substantive, because A. was being paid to do exactly what he was doing, as D.O. himself had pointed out in his evaluation of the proposal; but, rather, something *formal*, to make things *look* better. D.O. sent A. a letter asking, in effect, that the format be cleaned up and formalized!

A. was, of course, happy to comply, and a week later the "new look" report was mailed back, prettier than the old one but containing the same information. A few new touches were added, as for example the assurance that "no special difficulties have been encountered. The project is well on its way, as planned." We also learn the following good news: "Professor A. will visit with Professor K., world renowned authority on higher education [in Great Britain] to consult about our findings. No consulting fee is being charged by Professor K. and Professor A. will pay his own travel expenses." This is an incredible paragraph: "findings" that have never been revealed are alluded to; and we are assured that K. will not charge a fee for chatting with A., and that A. will not charge OE for this junket—as if this had been considered a possibility!

In mid-June of 1969, A. wrote a letter to OE containing two requests. The first of these was for an additional $6,000—"a small amount of supplementary funds"—to analyze data in the American Council on Education's newly operational data bank. Basically, the money was to pay for five weeks of a research analyst's time and two weeks for a programmer's time; for data processing; and for overhead and fee. There is no hint as to what kind of analysis is to be performed; nor is there any research plan at all. The second request is for more time:

Secondly, it seems advisable to extend the period of analysis for three months. This would mean that the final report would be submitted December 31, 1969. This additional time is required primarily because of two factors. First of all the relevant empirical relationships already encountered are more complex than originally anticipated. Secondly, researchers have been much more active in this field in the last year than it was possible to anticipate when the proposal was submitted. To cite only two examples, both the Carnegie Commission (under Clark Kerr) and HEW (under Alice Rivlin) have conducted extensive studies in this area and presented far-ranging policy proposals. It has been necessary to spend a considerable amount of time analyzing and evaluating these and other efforts, and relating them to our own work. Finally the analysis of the additional data from the ACE discussed in point one will require some extra time, though the additional three months of analysis seems required, however, even if supplemental funds are not available for analysis of the ACE data.

The reasoning is ingenuous. As we had already found out in the progress reports, A. was discovering the problems to be rather complex, something he just might have been expected to have known in advance. Also, as OE had been forewarned from the outset, A.'s study was not the only one in the field, to put it delicately, and his acquaintance with other work was minimal; so OE was paying him to find out what other people were doing, and now OE was being asked to extend the contract because A. had discovered that other people were doing a lot.

The June 30 progress report—mailed on June 27 (but in a project like this it could have been written almost any time)—repeated the substance of the above-cited letter, and reported a few developments. First, A. was slowly becoming more confident in his "tentative finding": "that federal aid—regardless of the form—aimed at enabling more lower class high school graduates to attend college would generally have less impact on the societal stratification structure (in terms of social mobility roles) than is generally assumed." This hazy and almost meaningless platitude could hardly have left OE gasping with amazement at A.'s powers of analysis and insight.

Second, the report tells what A. had been doing with most of his time: he had, during the April 1-June 30 period, "focused primarily on estimating the effects of federal aid on stimulating racial equality." When one compares A.'s sweeping plans, as outlined in his proposal, with this rather limited perspective, it becomes very evident that he was not doing anything near what he had originally said he would do. By now, OE would probably have had no trouble in cutting off further support of this abortive project, even given OE's loose management of it up to this point. But this was not to be.

A.'s request for more money and time must have rattled OE. D.O. took his time and asked for more explanation of the proposed "analysis" of ACE's data, as well as for a breakdown of two budget items: the salary item of $1,600 and the "data processing" item of $2,800. A. replied to this inquiry in a letter giving no details at all about the analysis, but carrying on at some length about how important the analysis is. As for the budget items, which cover $4,400 of the $6,000 asked for, A. broke them down into line form without explaining why each item was actually necessary.

Apparently it never occurred to anyone at OE to turn down A.'s request, so the extension and additional funds were granted. Another opéra-bouffe-style series of errors ensued in the course of this "small" additional award which, by the time it was over, must have cost a few thousand dollars in wasted man-hours. We will omit the minute details, which are spelled out in the documents.

Even this was not yet the end. In December, A. wrote for another extension, to March 31, 1970. The delay was entirely due to the slowness of receiving the ACE data, according to A.; he expected everything to be done by February at "the latest," but he was "asking for a delay until the end of March just to be on the safe side." The request was duly processed and granted by OE "at no additional cost to the government."

The report finally arrived in March 1970. It is authored by A. and his associate M. The Office of Education is nowhere mentioned; a reader would not know that OE funds had supported the project. The "Acknowledgments" page does not mention OE or a single person associated with OE or with the government.

What OE got was a very, very long (and wordy) essay, very, very short on hard data. At first sight, it looks as if OE got what it paid for: the thoughts of A. on the subject at hand. A closer look, however, reveals something very different.

To begin with, we find out that Part I was written by M., not A. (though we are assured that A. "freely exchanged ideas" with M., whatever that means). Now, Part I of the report is 191 pages long, more than half of the whole. It is to be questioned whether OE would have spent the money had it known that half the product was to be, after all, M.'s thoughts on the subject.

But at least M.'s thoughts are on the subject of the study! A.'s thoughts, on the other hand, as presented in the last 146 pages— some of which happened to be written by other people—are not on the subject of the contract at all. As it turned out, OE was subsidizing A., and a regal support staff, to do whatever A. pleased during—and quite a bit after—the year 1968-1969.

There is no record of any evaluation of the final report. A form letter from D.O., sent in June, accepted the report and approved final payment.

Specific Problems

This relatively modest case points up many of the specific problems we have earlier mentioned in general terms. On the government side, no one was really clear where the proposed study belonged, whether it should be made, or what program it properly fitted into. Over a dozen OE officials were involved at one point or another, but they were not in contact with each other on a regular basis and could not coordinate their activities. Errors and oversights were frequent. There were no clear guidelines concerning proper budgetary supervision or technical supervision; nor were there policies governing use of whatever findings might be produced. All in all, one gets the feeling that the Office of Education was hopelessly unaware of what the project was really all about, and had no mechanisms for keeping abreast of what was going on.

On the contractor's side, all the dilemmas are in evidence, albeit in miniature. What overhead and fee, if any, are appropriate? How is the value of thinking power to be measured? What is the line between flexibility and misrepresentation? When is a company performing a service, and when is it taking the government for a ride?

The problems encountered in the case I have just presented are by no means unusual. One company we have studied, a well-known private educational consulting firm, received over a million dollars' worth of contracts from the Office of Education and other federal agencies in about two years' time. What makes this statistic so significant is the fact that, at the outset of this period, the company was doing business at a total rate of only $250,000 a year from all sources, and had only one full-time professional employee! Naturally, this firm expanded rapidly and was helped in the process by an ingenious device; several proposals would be filed simultaneously, and the same names would appear on the various proposals as the investigators and researchers. As the proposals were funded, money became available to hire new staff—with the excess over 100 percent of any given person's time when the contributions from the various projects were added up.

Another firm we have looked into made a practice of submitting proposals with virtually no research design. This would make it difficult for OE personnel to know exactly what was to be expected in the project, and hence impossible for the government to monitor what was going on. Another regular practice of this firm was to promise mountains of data and accompanying analyses, and then to submit only the raw data, in the form of thousands and thousands of sheets of computer printouts. Since data in this form are virtually useless, the firm was then in a position to ask for additional funds for the analyses, and these funds would invariably be granted by a helpless and gullible OE. Although this happened repeatedly, no one at OE caught on to the pattern, and the firm enjoyed, and still enjoys, an excellent reputation.

Time and time again, firms have displayed a total disregard of deadlines and complete indifference to the importance of delivering results on time. In instance after instance, firms have asked for, and received, fees in addition to overhead charges, on the pretext that these fees were necessary to stimulate corporate stability and growth— as if these considerations are relevant to OE contracts and grants. Over and over, a project would be escalated into a far bigger activity than originally proposed or planned, with vast additional funds being allocated by OE through a noncompetitive, nonreviewed amendment procedure rather than through the normal process of funding approval. In one case we have studied, a project that OE thought might cost $75,000 was funded at $140,135 and was escalated through a series of amendments to $416,743—and it is still alive!

All the problems are by no means concentrated on the side of the contractor or grantee. The Office of Education, as provider of the funds and as the public agent responsible for their proper use, has plenty of its own problems. Our case studies are beginning to uncover a broad pattern of defective management throughout all phases of OE's activities—a dismal pattern that has been glimpsed in part by other study panels, but is only now being revealed in its full impact.

Consider, for example, the following partial list of defects that we have uncovered in OE's handling of contracts and grants during the preaward period alone:

1. Prearrangement seems to be the rule rather than the exception, in consideration of potential contractors and grantees. However an idea originates, it is apparently common practice for OE to discuss a project extensively with a favored award recipient, and to work out some sort of plan for proceeding. When this is done, the formalities are then instituted as an afterthought.

2. The intent of Congress is often disregarded by OE. Awards are often made with hardly a glance at the legislative intent of the program that has been authorized by Congress. It sometimes seems as if OE considers the total funds appropriated by Congress in any fiscal year as a big pool on which OE can draw at will for whatever programs it sees fit to fund.

3. Another failing prevalent in the early states of OE projects is the absence of carefully conceived specifications, work plans, or research design. This failing is evidenced both in OE-originated projects, where it is a critical flaw, and in outside-originated projects which have been discussed in advance with OE personnel.

4. Yet another virtually universal problem in proposals is the unavailability of solid budget information, a lack which OE does nothing to remedy. It is as if the very concept of budget justification is entirely alien to OE. The budgets are almost always descriptive line-item affairs presenting totals, with hardly a thought given to explaining *why* the particular item is necessary or *how* the money will be used to further the project. Indeed, we have seen many instances where the line-item description does not even correspond to the verbal description given in the text of the proposal! OE virtually never attempts to clarify the budgets or force an adequate explanation prior to the award.

5. Evaluation procedures are slipshod and erratic. Sometimes there is no evaluation at all. Sometimes there are a few in-house evaluations. Sometimes there are a few outside evaluations. There seems to be no rhyme or reason to the process, no pattern at all. But worst of all, OE has no discernible policy concerning what ought to be done with an evaluation once they get it. There seems to be no connection at all between the content of evaluations and further subsequent actions by OE.

6. A particularly disturbing feature of the award procedure is the seeming determination of OE to spend all the money that has been appropriated. In the few cases where contracts are put out for bids, it is a foregone conclusion that someone will get the award, even if no one has submitted a really satisfactory proposal. Similarly, when prearranged proposals come in, there is an almost inexorable drive to fund them, regardless of their defects. All this becomes even more evident as the end of the fiscal year approaches, when more and more projects are frenetically rushed through in order to commit all available funds. No one at OE seems to feel that congressional appropriations are (except where otherwise indicated, in explicit language) *upper* ceilings on permissible expenditures, and that public moneys should not be spent on unworthy projects.

The defects listed above form but a small part of the whole picture. Many additional problems arise during the award period and after the project is completed. What we are finding is the simple absence of good management, or virtually any management at all, at OE. The implications of this situation are truly staggering when one contemplates the important, indeed central, role that OE plays in the educational affairs of virtually every community in the nation.

Some Hard Questions

The first major set of questions must relate to the structure of the federal government. We must ask candidly, and repeatedly, what form of agency and departmental organization can best serve the needs of our government today? What overlapping jurisdictions need to be separated, what conflicting authorities have to be resolved? What principles of management must be introduced to ensure that public funds are being spent in a reasonable manner?

These questions are only beginning to be asked now, and they are scarcely being posed with a sense of urgency that the situation calls for. Unless they are asked and answered soon, we will be engulfed and overburdened with a runaway federal program—a diverse, overlapping, unplanned, confusing array of governmental efforts whose faults are beyond remedy and whose abuses are beyond belief.

The second major set of questions centers upon the rampant commercialism that threatens to dominate the educational scene. Will the lucrative contract or grant become the new mark of academic success, to replace the traditional measures of teaching skill, scholarship, and humanity? Will the high fee be tomorrow's school prize? Will the wisdom of educators be turned to outfoxing government agencies, and finding ways to make short deliveries on long promises, instead of being turned to shortening the path to truth? Will the educator devote his energies to luring the government into surrendering funds, instead of pursuing his scholarly and pedagogical interests?

The whole question of the relation of profits to social betterment must be examined. It is not simply, "Are profits in this area bad?" but "What should profits in this area look like? Which are acceptable, and which are not acceptable? What are we getting for our money?"

There is no doubt that much value can be realized by the efforts of private companies and individual investigators. The private sector is richly populated with those who honestly offer the service of their companies in the solution of social problems feeling that they can do it better because they know better, and feeling also that they can make a legitimate profit and feel comfortable about it because the results *really have* produced a better society in some respect, no matter how small.

We should not allow ourselves to be deluded by categorization of companies into "profit-making" and "nonprofit." Sometimes we act as if "nonprofit" organizations are morally superior because somehow they are doing the job out of some high moral ideal—as if somehow it was immoral to make a profit. In fact, any organization has to receive enough income to cover its outgo, or it goes out of business. The only real differences between corporations usually classified as "profit-making" and those classified as "nonprofit" is that the former require a profit as a return on equity advanced by stockholders in the form of money, while the latter require a "profit" as return on equity advanced by members in the form of skills. In a corporation a profit is distributed as dividends to the stockholders; in a nonprofit association a profit is distributed to the controlling members as increased salaries, or in the form of other fringe benefits and improvements.

To summarize, then, there are two central concepts involved here: (1) the inefficiency, confusion, waste, breakdown, and corruption (active or passive) of the federal bureaucracy; (2) the inefficiency, confusion, waste, breakdown, and corruption (active or passive) of the private technocratic bureaucracy. And the big questions before us are the following:

1. What can Congress and people honestly expect from big business, or from the federal agencies, in answering social needs?

2. What price are we willing to pay private industry for its expertise?

3. How richly are we willing to subsidize the development of expertise? How do we gauge what is fair here?

4. How do we identify industrial parasites when they surface, and how might we control their growth?

5. What are some parallels in the development of the "rampant rise in commercialism" on the part of professional educators and the rise of the profiteers in the poverty-education arena who are in private industry? Is there a connection between the two?

These questions cry for answers. Soon. Before education is taken irreversibly out of the hands of educators and placed in the hands of managers and entrepreneurs.

A study in 1971 by the General Accounting Office concluded that the management system used for research and evaluation contracts by the Office of Education was inadequate and that the contract officers did not have the competence required for managing contracts of this kind.[2]

Why the Review Was Made

The Office of Education has entered into contracts for studies and evaluations of federal educational programs to determine whether these programs are meeting their objectives. The information obtained is used in the development, design, and management of the programs and to inform educators about the programs.

The studies are performed by public or private agencies, organizations, groups, or individuals.

The General Accounting Office (GAO) reviewed the Office of Education's administration of these contracts to determine whether its policies and procedures were adequate for ensuring that the information obtained was useful and provided the benefits intended.

GAO identified eighty-six study and evaluation contracts, totaling about $22,000,000, which had completion dates after January 1, 1969. Of these contracts, GAO selected twenty-four for review. At the time of GAO's review, fourteen of the contracts had been completed at a cost of $2,200,000. The remaining ten contracts were still in progress and were estimated to cost about $9,100,000.

Findings and Conclusions

Office of Education officials considered the information produced by five of the fourteen completed studies to be of limited use. The cost of the five studies ($935,000) represented 41.6 percent of the total cost of the fourteen completed contracts.

The results of the nine other completed contracts were considered by the Office of Education to be adequate and useful.

Two of the ten ongoing studies may also fall short of meeting their objectives.

—A study, costing $542,000, to evaluate curriculum for the environmentally deprived child probably will not meet the objectives set by the Office of Education.

—A $7,000,000 contract to study the Follow Through program may not produce the information desired unless the Office of Education clarifies the objectives of the study.

Numerous problems were encountered with some of the studies.

—Certain of the studies lacked sufficient research, test data, and analyses to support their conclusions.

—One contained little or no original data; another contained inaccurate data.

Weaknesses in the administration of the contracts contributed to the failure of these studies to produce the desired results.

In a number of instances, the contractors' descriptions of work to be performed were not specific enough to ensure that the work performed would provide the Office of Education with useful information. Written agreements were not obtained on significant changes in the work. Also contracts were not monitored closely enough to keep responsible Office of Education officials informed on a contractor's progress.

Under such circumstances it is difficult to hold the contractors responsible for poor performance.

The following two examples illustrate the poor administrative practices of the Office of Education.

—Office of Education officials concluded that research conducted under a $103,000 contract was performed poorly and that the final report contained many unsubstantiated statements. GAO attributes the poor results to a lack of specific contract objectives.

—Office of Education officials concluded that the report produced under a $200,000 contract lacked sufficient data or research findings to be of value. GAO believes that this resulted because the Office of Education did not formally amend the contract to include work it considered important.

If the Office of Education is to receive the benefits intended from study and evaluation contracts, improvements are needed in the administration of these contracts.

At the close of GAO's review, the Department of Health, Education, and Welfare (HEW) was preparing a guide for its project monitors, which was to deal with many of the problem areas discussed in this report. GAO believes that the guide can result in a significant improvement.

Recommendations or Suggestions

In preparing the guide for project monitors, the secretary of HEW should provide for inclusion of:

—Guidance to help ensure that the objectives and requirements of contracts are clearly understood by the contractors and that the scope of work is described in sufficient detail in the contract.

—The methods to be used in monitoring the contractor's progress such as required site visits at specified points in the contract period.

—Criteria for use by agency personnel in evaluating a final report prior to acceptance to determine whether the contract objectives have been satisfied.

—The steps required to be taken when considering action against a contractor for poorly performed work, including consultation with legal counsel and contracting officials.

In addition, the secretary should provide for the establishment of an orientation course to acquaint agency program personnel involved in the administration of study and evaluation contracts with the requirements of Federal Procurement Regulations and agency instructions.

This critique recognized management inadequacies that the General Accounting Office suggests can at least be partly overcome by the establishment of an orientation course to acquaint agency program personnel with the requirements of federal procurement regulations and agency instructions. Lack of such knowledge, however, is not the only limitation in the background of some contract officers. Some have little understanding of the functioning of education in schools and colleges; its major objectives; the roles of teachers and administrators; the influences of home, community, and peer groups on children's attitudes and behavior; and the differences between short periods of specific learning and the continuing sequential learning experiences provided in schools and colleges. Some seem to conceive of the classroom as a psychological rather than a human ecosystem. Others view the school as a place where education is delivered rather than an environment in which active children and youth with purposes of their own are stimulated and encouraged to learn what the school seeks to teach.

Those contract officers whose perceptions of the enterprise of schooling are faulty are not able to monitor appropriately the research, development, and evaluation activities that are undertaken to increase understanding and to guide improvement of school programs. It is claimed by some university officials that the contract officers assigned to medical research and development seem to have a more accurate conception of the work of health agencies than those assigned to educational research and development projects have of educational institutions.

The mistakes and shortcomings of educational research and development activities during the recent past can be overcome. They are not inherent in the nature of the field. Their existence, however, has been widely publicized, and the layman's faith and hope in the contribution of educational research and development to the improvement of education have greatly diminished. Prospects for the future will be influenced by this change in view.

Notes

1. Edith Green, "Federal Funds in Education: When Does Use Become Abuse?" *Educational Forum* 36 (November 1971): 7-20.

2. Comptroller General of the United States, *Need for Improving the Administration of Study and Evaluation Contracts* (Washington, D.C.: U.S. General Accounting Office, 1971).

5. IMPROVING THE QUALITY
OF EDUCATIONAL RESEARCH

Several of the points emphasized in Chapters 3 and 4 deal directly or indirectly with the quality of educational research, and some suggestions were made for steps to be taken to improve quality. From these and other sources seven kinds of recommendations were found: concentrate support on highly competent researchers; improve the competence of those conducting research; recruit into educational research highly qualified researchers from other disciplines who could help to illuminate educational problems; select research projects and programs much more carefully; construct several appropriate conceptual models of educational phenomena to guide research so that knowledge can be accumulated; develop better management and support systems for educational research activities; establish a critical review apparatus for the field of educational research.

The argument for concentrating support on highly competent researchers was presented briefly in Chapter 4 and will not be restated here. Proposals for improving the preparation of those engaged in educational research have been made in several recent publications. In 1966 a study of training for educational research found several serious limitations in the programs commonly followed and recommended major improvements.[1] The Committee on Educational Research of the National Academy of Education drew upon this California study and several others in making the following recommendations:[2]

Recommendations

The training of educational researchers should not be the un-
divided responsibility of schools of education. This conclusion is
reached by many within the educational field. It stands out among
the recommendations of the Buswell-McConnell study, recommendations reached after discussion with experienced educational research
workers. The fact that several of the discussants had been high officers
of the American Educational Research Association, and that others
were or had been deans of schools of education, eliminates any
question of adverse bias.

Certain features are likely to characterize any superior program of
training for research on education. These include (1) full-time study
for three consecutive years, preferably at an early age; (2) training as
part of a student group individually and collectively dedicated to
research careers; (3) participation in research, at a steadily advancing
level of responsibility, starting in the first year of graduate school if
not earlier; (4) a thorough grounding in at least one academic discipline, together with solid training in whatever technical skills that
discipline employs; and (5) study of the educational process and
educational institutions, bringing into a single perspective the social
goals of education, the bases on which policy decisions are made, the
historical development of the curriculum, the nature of the learner,
and other factors.

Of these features, only the fifth has been at all common in the
training of doctoral students in education. In the past, graduate
faculties in education have recruited students for research training
mainly among the teachers who attend summer sessions. These
teachers tend to be interested in practical recommendations and in
advancement to higher posts within school systems. When a research
worker is recruited from this pool, he may have completed half his
graduate study before he starts to view himself as a prospective investigator, with all the change of intellectual style that implies. He may
well be thirty-five or older when he makes the shift. Yet in nearly
every scientific field it has been observed that an investigator does
his most creative work before age thirty-five. In most schools of
education the doctoral students committed to doing research are
outnumbered at least three to one by those who regard the doctoral
dissertation as the one piece of research of their lifetimes, as no

more than an academic exercise. The graduate student in education is likely to participate in research (apart from his dissertation) only if hired as an assistant, and then may carry out routine activities designed to serve the project rather than activities that contribute to his development. Education has no tradition of the undergraduate honors work that other fields use to give students an early taste of inquiry. In a scientific or technical field the graduate student almost always enters with an undergraduate major in a science or mathematics. In education, entering graduate students may have no more intellectual preparation for research than the one or two science courses that meet minimum standards for a bachelor's degree.

We must not fail to acknowledge the bright exceptions within this gloomy picture. Many schools of education have a few young students who enter with top records in undergraduate psychology, mathematics, chemistry, or the like, shifting to educational research because they are challenged by its immediate relevance to the world and its emphasis on integrated knowledge rather than on isolated specializations. No doubt there are ten times as many such students who could be recruited . . . .

Whereas formerly there were few opportunities for research careers, and few students seeking them, the better schools of education now can have enough research trainees to warrant a distinct program. The program needs to be special; adding isolated courses and apprenticeships will not suffice. The research trainee cannot be left to select most of his courses from a catalogue designed for the practitioner. He cannot be left without the continual interaction with other inquiry-minded students that is one of the great strengths of graduate departments. For this reason, research trainees within schools of education should be treated as a distinct group and given special opportunities to interact with data, with each other, with experienced research workers, and with students applying similar research methods to noneducational problems. Buswell and McConnell go so far as to recommend a degree-granting institute for research training in education, formally outside the school of education though sharing some of its staff. Separatism can go too far, if it removes the research trainees from all communication with those who have the practitioner's interests. Through such contacts the researcher can learn about field problems deserving his attention, and the practitioner can gain respect for the research worker's style of thinking. Many

different programs can be designed that have the desired characteristics; which structure is best will depend on the field of study, the
university, and the individual student.

The movement of the past two decades toward a full-time student
body in graduate schools of education has brought developments
that need to be reexamined. Full-time students are a delight to the
faculty, but they have to be supported. The advent of research
grants that could pay half-time salaries to students was enthusiastically
welcomed, and it was rightly seen that these assistantships provide a
training superior to the old mixture of courses and completely
independent work. But when funds are granted to carry out a
particular piece of the professor's research, the student's interests
have to be subordinated to the requirements of the contract. Just
because the work has to be done, he may find himself running subjects or feeding data into the computer long after the work has
ceased to have educative value for him . . . . The proper program will
provide the student with the apprenticeships and collaborative experience he needs, but it will not enslave him to a project. Very
likely schools of education will need to engage nonstudents with
technical skills to carry on the noneducative chores on which a fair
proportion of every research budget is necessarily spent.

Positive leadership will be required to develop training programs
that make adequate use of the academic disciplines relevant to education, and that leadership will have to come from schools of education. Only in isolated cases can one expect another department to
take the initiative in organizing training for work on education. It is
noteworthy that very few of the research training programs supported
by the Office of Education are based in departments outside schools
of education, though such proposals have been officially encouraged.
Leaders within education faculties will have to learn how the basic
fields can illuminate educational concerns, and will have to survey
their own campuses to identify departments that are likely to enter
into collaborative training. Training programs must spread into disciplines other than psychology and statistics, the two that have long
collaborated with educators. The list of conventional social sciences
does not exhaust the possibilities that should be exploited. Relevant
interests are emerging in economic systems analysis, in linguistics and
in subspecialties of psycholinguistics and sociolinguistics, and elsewhere.

The argument for recruiting highly qualified researchers in other disciplines to engage their talents in studies that help in understanding educational problems is not new. It is, in fact, similar to the argument made in the field of medical research for involving researchers from other disciplines such as biochemistry, genetics, and molecular biology to help in understanding medical problems. Our knowledge of education has been greatly aided by such studies as those of psychologists relating to learning, of sociologists relating to the effects of social class, of economists relating to the economic values of education in the formation of "human capital," and of political scientists relating to the "politics of education." Since education is central to any modern society and its culture, it seems obvious that scholars and scientists who are studying the various facets of society and culture can develop knowledge about educational problems if their attention is directed toward this area.

One recent effort to recruit excellent researchers from various disciplines was undertaken by the Committee on Basic Research in Education.[3] This interdisciplinary committee was established in 1968 by the National Academy of Education and the National Academy of Sciences at the request of R. Louis Bright, then associate commissioner for research in the Office of Education, to recommend expenditures on basic research projects. Appointed for three years, it was to assist the Office of Education in developing a program of basic research. One of its major objectives was to attract the attention of competent scholars and scientists from various disciplines who might not otherwise be disposed to devote their energies to basic studies on education.

The committee considered its activities highly successful. Its major grant program supported both ongoing and new research by established researchers in many disciplines. The small grant program encouraged forty-one promising young researchers to begin projects in areas that are relevant to education. In many cases research was begun that would not otherwise have been supported, and individuals who had not previously addressed themselves to basic research in education were attracted to this field. The committee conducted research workshops that helped not only to define many new problems of interest to education, but also widened the circle of researchers from a number of disciplines.

The selection of research projects and programs is critical to any effort to obtain significant knowledge. The quality of research is greatly influenced by the kinds of questions on which the study is focused and the strategy employed in the investigation. Though the initial formulation is largely the work of the investigator, the decision to provide supporting funds is the responsibility of the granting agency. A report of the House Committee on Government Operations gives an unfavorable evaluation of the quality of research sponsored by the Office of Education,[4] whereas the National Science Foundation and the National Institutes of Health receive high ratings. The National Academy of Education's

Committee on Educational Research outlines the problems involved in the selection of projects: [5]

The decisions of the Office of Education regarding allocations of research funds are much criticized in the scholarly community. Panels, when used, have sometimes been overloaded to the point where panel members were unable to make informed decisions. In other instances panels have felt that the staff was overimpressed by the social significance the work would have if successful, and did not understand the reviewer's reservations regarding the quality of the proposed work. Staff members involved in the review process have generally been in poor communication with the academic sector, showing more interest in the topical urges of the moment than in the solid development of knowledge. This is in part a reflection of pressure from elected officials and the schools, in part a symptom of staff overload, and in part a problem of staff recruiting.

Congressional pressures on the allocation of research funds demonstrate a misunderstanding of the research process. We have urged one cardinal principle for research support: *a study is worth undertaking only if it will be truly disciplined and hence capable of giving solid results.* But we find a congressional committee urging that the Bureau of Research assign a far larger responsibility in the review of research proposals to consultants employed in elementary and secondary schools. With all respect for the contributions such individuals can make to the knowledge of the OE about current problems of the schools, we cannot equate this with a competence to review proposals. In the course of service on panels of the OE, several members of this committee have tried to make use of reviews by educators in the field to whom research proposals were sent for comment. Such educators make little contribution to proposal review because they do not discriminate between immediacy and relevance; considerations of discipline, depth, and long-range significance are neglected.

An overemphasis on immediacy is seen also in the congressional concern[6] that the research projects to which funds are allocated are not in one-to-one correspondence with the action programs of the OE. An action program to help poor children, or to improve foreign-language teaching, or whatever, is legislated by Congress only when some problem rises to the crisis stage. Action, once decreed, is mounted with a rapidity that leaves no scope for proper conclusion-oriented research and all too often leaves none for orderly developmental research. If research is to make a major contribution, it must begin long before a crash program is authorized. Hence there should be a positive effort to identify problem areas that are still below the horizon of legislation and action, rather than for an allocation policy that instructs research workers to bring up the rear after the action starts. To be sure, research should go on in areas where there are action programs, but a good deal of that research should be aimed to provide insights that will be useful in mounting second- and third-generation programs, rather than to provide hasty and partial answers to the questions of the current year.

Credit can be given to the Bureau of Research for efforts to identify problem areas that are outside current fashion. There are serious risks in a policy of "directed research" if a central agency channels research effort without a well-developed sense as to which problems are likely to yield to disciplined inquiry. On the other hand, the agency is not doing its duty if it does not call the practically salient problems to the attention of scholars, so that the scholars will seriously consider whether their techniques of inquiry can and should be turned into those channels. The allocation of resources must in the end be a joint effort of the community of investigators and the mission-oriented agency. Neither can "direct," but both can lead. The negotiating process should be a mutual education, so that all participants will see the final allocations as both sound and potentially relevant.

Perhaps the most important recommendation we can suggest to the Office of Education is that it find better channels for frank communication with the scholarly community. Many communications that come from the OE suggest a lack of understanding of the values and thought processes of the academic world. This gap persists, despite the fact that a reasonable proportion of the staff members have fine academic qualifications and experience (usually, however, limited to schools of education). Something in the institutional pattern seems to isolate them and distort their language. Most applicants are hesitant to criticize a potential source of funds, and persons holding contracts feel diffident about acknowledging their troubles to OE monitors who have failed to establish a colleaguelike relationship. Consequently, the OE does not know which of its rulings, policies, and practices alienate and impede the investigator.

The development of scientific knowledge through the work of many in-dividuals and groups involves the organization of questions and findings so that it is possible to keep building in a cumulative way. Each new investigation need not start from scratch, but can use what has been constructed in the past and add new understanding. It is often claimed that educational research projects have rarely been based on substantial bodies of organized knowledge, and raw empiricism takes the place of theory in guiding investigations. In his presidential address to the American Educational Research Association at its Chicago meet-ing in 1974, Patrick Suppes argued for giving more attention to theory:[7]

Why Theory?

There are five kinds of argument I would like to examine that can be used to make the case for the relevance of theory to educational research. The first is an argument by analogy, the second is in terms of the reorganization of experience, the third is as a device for recog-nizing complexity, the fourth is a comparison with Deweyan prob-lem solving, and the fifth concerns the triviality of bare empiricism. I now turn to each of these arguments.

Argument by Analogy

The success of theory in the natural sciences is recognized by everyone. More recently, some of the social sciences, especially economics and psychology in certain parts, have begun to achieve considerable theoretical developments. It is argued that the obvious and universally recognized importance of theory in the more mature sciences is strong evidence for the universal generalization that theory is important in all sciences, and, consequently, we have an argument by analogy for the importance of theory in educational research.

However, since at least the eleventh century, when Anselm tried to use an argument by analogy to prove the existence of God, there is proper skepticism that an argument by analogy carries much weight. Although the argument that the success of the natural sciences in the use of theory provides an excellent example for educational research, it does not follow that theory must be comparably useful as we move from one subject to the other.

Reorganization of Experience

A more important way to think about the role of theory is to attack directly the problem of identifying the need for theory in a subject matter. In all cases where theory has been successful in science I think we can make an excellent argument for the deeper organization of experience the theory has thereby provided. A powerful theory changes our perspective on what is important and what is superficial. Perhaps the most striking example in the history of physics is the law of inertia, which says that a body shall continue uniformly in its direction of motion until acted upon by some external force. Aristotle and other ancient natural philosophers were persuaded that the evidence of experience is clear: A body does *not* continue in motion unless it is acted upon by force. We can all agree that our own broad experience is exactly that of Aristotle's. It was a deep insight and represented a radical reorganization of how to think about the world to recognize that the theory of motion is correctly expressed by laws like that of inertia and seldom by our direct commonsense experience.

A good example in education of the impact of theory on reorganizing our way of thinking about our discipline is the infusion of economic theory that has taken place in the last decade with such vigor and impact.[8] The attempt, for instance, to develop an economic theory of productivity for our schools can be criticized in many different ways, but it still remains that we have been forced to think anew about the allocation of resources, especially of how we can develop a deeper running theory for the efficient allocation of resources to increase productivity and, at the same time, to develop a better theory for the measurements of input and output and the construction of production functions.

Let me give one example from some of my own discussions with economists, especially with Dean Jamison. Starting from the economists' way of looking at output, it is natural to ask how we can measure the output of an elementary school, for example. What I find striking is the lack of previous discussion of this problem in the literature of education.[9] Even if we restrict ourselves to measurements of academic skills, and indeed only to the academic skills assessed on standard achievement tests, we still have the problem of how to aggregate the measurement of these skills to give us an overall measure of output. If one accepts the fact, as most of us do, that academic achievement alone is not important, but that a variety of social and personal skills, as well as the development of a sense of values and of moral autonomy, are needed, one is really nonplussed by even crude assessments of these individual components. There is, of course, the well-worn answer that the things that matter most are really ineffable and immeasurable, but this romantic attitude is not one for which I have much tolerance. I am simply struck in my own thinking by the difficulty of making a good assessment, and my sense of the difficulties has been put in focus by trying to deal with some of the theoretical ideas economists have brought to bear in education.

Recognition of Complexity

One of the thrusts of theory is to show that what appear on the surface to be simple matters of empirical investigation, on a deeper view, prove to be complex and subtle. The basic skills of language and mathematics at any level of instruction, but primarily at the most elementary level, provide good examples. If we are offered two methods of reading it is straightforward to design an experiment to see whether or not a difference of any significant magnitude between the two methods can be found in the achievement of students. It has been progress in education to recognize that such problems can be studied as scientific problems, and it is a mark of the work of the first half of this century, the *golden age* of empiricism as I termed it earlier, to firmly establish the use of such methods in education. It is an additional step, however, and one in which the recognition of theory is the main carrier of progress to recognize that the empirical comparison of two methods of teaching reading or of teaching subtraction, to take an example that has been much researched, is by no means to provide anything like the theory of how the child learns to read or learns to do arithmetic.

A most elementary perusal of psychological considerations of information processing shows at once how far we are from an adequate theory of learning even the most elementary basic skills. It is a requirement of theory, but not of experimentalism, to provide analysis of the process by which the child acquires a basic skill and later uses it. It is a merit of theory to push for a deeper understanding of the acquisition and not to rest until we have a complete process analysis of what the child does and what goes on inside his head as he acquires a new skill.

The history of physics can be written around the concept of the search for mechanisms ranging from the reduction of astronomical motions to compositions of circular motions in the time of Ptolemy to the gravitational and electromagnetic mechanisms of modern physics. It has been to a partial extent, and should be to a greater extent, a primary thrust of theory in educational research to seek mechanisms or processes that answer the question of why a given aspect of education works the way it does. This should be true whether we consider the individual learning of a child beginning school or the much broader interaction between adolescents, their peer groups, and what is supposed to take place in their high school classrooms. For educational purposes we need an understanding of biosocial mechanisms of influence as much as in medicine we need an understanding of biochemical mechanisms for the control of disease in a host organism. The search beyond the facts for a conception of mechanism or of explanation forces upon us a recognition of the complexity of the phenomena and the need for a theory of this complexity.

Why Not Deweyan Problem Solving?

The instrumental view of knowledge developed by Peirce and Dewey led, especially in the hands of Dewey, to an emphasis on the importance of problem solving in inquiry. As Dewey repeatedly emphasized, inquiry is the transformation of an indeterminate situation that presents a problem into one that is determinate and unified by the solution of the initial problem. Dewey's conception of inquiry can be regarded as a proper corrective to an overly scholastic and rigid conception of scientific theory, but the weakness of replacing classical conceptions of scientific theory by inquiry as problem solving is that the articulation of the historically and intellectually important role of theory in inquiry is neglected or slighted. In any case, even if we accept some of Dewey's criticisms of classical philosophical conceptions of theory, we can argue for the importance of the development of scientific theories as potential tools for use in problem solving. It would be a naive and careless view of problem solving to think that on each occasion where we find ourselves in an indeterminate situation we can begin afresh to think about the problem and not to bring to bear a variety of sophisticated systematic tools. This sounds so obvious that it is hard to believe anyone could disagree with it. Historically, however, it is important to recognize that under the influence of Dewey educational leadership moved away from development and testing of theory, and Dewey himself did not properly recognize the importance of deep-running systematic theories.[10]

The newest version of the naive problem-solving viewpoint is to be found in the romantics running from John Holt to Charles Silberman, who seem to think that simply by using our natural intuition and by observing what goes on in classrooms we can put together all the ingredients needed to solve our educational problems. To a large extent these new romantics are the proper heirs of Dewey, and they suffer from the same intellectual weakness—the absence of the felt need for theoretically based techniques of analysis.

The continual plague of romantic problem solvers in education will only disappear, as have plagues of the past, when the proper antidotes are developed. My belief about these antidotes is that we need deeprunning theories of the kind that have driven alchemists out of chemistry and astrologers out of astromomy.

Triviality of Bare Empiricism

The best general argument for theory in educational research I have left for last. This is the obvious triviality of bare empiricism as an approach to knowledge. Those parts of science that have been beset by bare empiricism have suffered accordingly. It is to be found everywhere historically, ranging from the sections on natural history in the early *Transactions of the Royal Society* of the seventeenth century to the endless lists of case histories in medicine, or as an example closer to home, to studies of methods of instruction that report only raw data. At its most extreme level, bare empiricism is simply the recording of individual facts, and, with no apparatus of generalization or theory, these bare facts duly recorded lead nowhere. They do not provide even a practical guide for future experience or policy. They do not provide methods of prediction or analysis. In short, bare empiricism does not generalize.

The same triviality may be claimed for the bare intuition of the romantics. Either bare empiricism or bare intuition leads not only to triviality, but also to chaos in practice if each teacher is left only to his or her own observations and intuitions. Reliance on bare empiricism or bare intuition in educational practice is a mental form of streaking, and nudity of mind is not as appealing as nudity of body . . . .

Sources of Theory

I promised earlier to examine the more general question of whether theory in educational research is chiefly a matter of applying theories developed in economics, psychology, sociology, anthropology, and other sciences close in spirit to the central problems of education. I firmly believe that such applications will continue to play a major role in educational research as they have in the past, but I also resist the notion that theoretically based work in educational research must wait for the latest developments in various other scientific disciplines before it can move forward. Other areas of applied science show a much more complicated and tangled history of interaction between the basically applied discipline and the fundamental discipline nearest to it. Physics is not just applied mathematics; nor is electrical engineering just applied physics. These disciplines interact and mutually enrich each other. The same can be said for education.

In the earlier history of this century it was difficult to disentangle progress in educational psychology from progress in more general experimental psychology, and recently some of the best young economists have claimed the economics of education as the primary area of economics in which they will develop their fundamental contributions. The role of educational researchers should be not merely to test theories made by others, but, when the occasion demands and the opportunity is there, to create new theories as well. Some areas, like the theory of instruction, seem ripe for this sort of development. Another area that I like to call the theory of talking and listening, or, what we might call in more standard terms, the theory of verbal communication, seems ripe also for developments special to education, and I do not propose that we wait for linguists and logicians to set us on the right theoretical tracks. What is important is not the decision as to whether the theories should be made at home or abroad, but the positive decision to increase significantly the theory-laden character of our research.

Another point needs to be made about these matters of the source of theory. One of the favorite economic generalizations of our time is that this is the age of specialization. Not every man can do everything equally well, as most of us know when faced with the breakdown of a television set or a washing machine or some other modern device of convenience. This same attitude of specialization should be our attitude toward theory. Not everyone should have the same grasp of theory nor the same involvement in its development. Physics has long recognized such a division of labor between experimental and theoretical physics, and I have come to believe that we need to encourage a similar division in educational research. Ultimately, the most important work may be empirical, but we need both kinds of workers in the vineyard, and we need variety of training for these various workers, not only in terms of different areas of education, but also in terms of whether their approach is primarily theoretical or experimental. It is a mark of the undeveloped character of current educational research that we do not have as much division of labor and specialization of research technique as seems desirable.

According to one apocryphal story about the late John von Neumann, he was asked in the early 1950s to put together a master list of unsolved problems in mathematics comparable to the famous list given by Hilbert at the beginning of the century. Von Neumann answered that he did not know enough about the various branches of mathematics as they had then developed to provide such a list. I shall be happy when the same kind of developments are found in educational research, and when not only inquiring reporters but also colleagues across the hall recognize that the theoretical work in learning theory, or theories of instruction, or the economics of education, or what have you, is now too richly developed and too intricate to have more than amateur opinions about it.

It is often thought and said that what we most need in education is wisdom and broad understanding of the issues that confront us. Not at all, I say. What we need are deeply structured theories in education that drastically reduce, if not eliminate, the need for wisdom. I do not want wise men to design or build the airplane I fly in, but rather technical men who understand the theory of aerodynamics and the structural properties of metal. I do not want a banker acting like a sage to recommend the measures to control inflation, but rather an economist who can articulate a theory that will be shown to work and who can make explicit the reason why it works (or fails). And so it is with education. Wisdom we need, I will admit, but good theories we need even more. I want to see a new generation of trained theorists and an equally competent band of experimentalists to surround them, and I look for the day when they will show that the theories I now cherish were merely humble way stations on the road to the theoretical palaces they have constructed.

Mrs. Green's article, the recommendations of the General Accounting Office, and the comments presented earlier from the report of the committee of the National Academy of Education are sufficient to indicate the need for developing a better management and support system for educational research activities. At this stage such a recommendation cannot be accompanied by citations of highly effective systems. The universities, regional laboratories, and research development centers recognize the problems, but have yet to test promising solutions. We can be sure, however, that the prospects of educational R and D in the future will be affected by the appropriateness and effectiveness of the management and support systems that will develop.

Research in other fields depends heavily for the maintenance of quality on the critical review apparatus that has been developed in each field. Every major research effort is subject to examination and critical comment by other scholars and scientists. This review includes all facets deemed important, such as the questions posed, the data and the methods of collecting them, the methods of analysis and interpretation, the relevance and plausibility of the findings, and so forth. Such a critical review apparatus has not yet been established in the field of educational research. The Review of Educational Research *and the* Encyclopedia of Educational Research *are summaries of findings of investigations, not critical reviews of their quality. When the field of educational research develops a critical review apparatus that is applied to important projects, and to programs of research in various areas, it is likely that the quality of educational research will be improved. At that time the critical reviews will furnish examples of quality standards, and many researchers will seek to meet the standards that differentiate "good research" from that which is mediocre or poor.*

When we look to the future we must realize that the improvement of the quality of educational research appears fully as important as obtaining adequate funds to expand its quantity.

Notes

1. Guy T. Buswell and T. R. McConnell, *Training for Educational Research* (Berkeley, Calif.: Center for the Study of Higher Education, University of California, Berkeley, 1966).

2. *Research for Tomorrow's Schools,* ed. Lee J. Cronbach and Patrick Suppes (New York: Macmillan, 1969), 212-214, 216-218.

3. *Final Report of the Committee on Basic Research in Education* (Washington, D.C.: Division of Behavioral Sciences, National Academy of Sciences—National Research Council, 1972).

4. House Committee on Government Operations, *The Use of Social Research in Federal Domestic Programs* (Washington, D.C.: U.S. Government Printing Office, 1967).

5. *Research for Tomorrow's Schools,* ed. Cronbach and Suppes, 249-251.

6. House Special Subcommittee on Education, *Study of the United States Office of Education* (Washington, D.C.: U.S. Government Printing Office, 1967), 209 ff.

7. Patrick Suppes, "The Place of Theory in Educational Research," *Educational Researcher* 3 (June 1974): 4-6, 8-9.

8. A good survey is to be found in *Economics of Education: Selected Readings,* 2 vols., ed. Mark Blaug (Harmondsworth, Middlesex, England: Penguin Books, 1968-1969).

9. Exceptions are E. B. Page, "Seeking a Measure of General Educational Advancement: The Bentee," *Journal of Educational Measurement* 9 (Spring 1972): 33-43; and E. B. Page and T. F. Breen III, "Educational Values for Measurement Technology: Some Theory and Data," in *Frontiers of Educational Measurement and Information Systems,* ed. W. E. Coffman (Boston: Houghton Mifflin, 1973).

10. The most detailed expression of John Dewey's view of scientific inquiry as problem solving is to be found in his *Logic, the Theory of Inquiry* (New York: Holt, 1938). A critical, but I think not unsympathetic, analysis of this work is to be found in Patrick Suppes, "Nagel's Lectures on Dewey's Logic," in *Philosophy, Science, and Method,* ed. Sidney Morgenbesser, Patrick Suppes, and Morton G. White (New York: St. Martin's Press, 1969).

6. RELEVANCE AND IMPLEMENTATION OF DEVELOPMENT ACTIVITIES

Chapter 5 dealt with the improvement of research. This chapter discusses certain problems of educational development and suggestions for improvements in that area. In the past, some knowledge gained from research in one generation became part of the cognitive map of the educator in the next generation and thus served to orient and guide his activities. This process has seemed too slow and indirect as a basis for the improvement of practice in schools and colleges. Various policies have been adopted during the last twenty years in the hope of connecting research and development more directly with educational practice and speeding up the applications of relevant knowledge. Two recent reports have presented interpretations of experience with these policies and have made proposals for improvement.

The first of these was a memorandum of November 1973 published by the Stanford Center for Research and Development in Teaching. The authors found a gulf between teachers and administrators on one side and researchers on the other, a gulf created both by mythical beliefs and by real differences. But they also found successful linkages between the two groups, as the following excerpt from the memorandum shows: [1]

Linking Strategies

To this point the discussion has centered around the barriers between researchers and their field users. On a more optimistic note, however, our research revealed a number of successful "linking strategies," organizational practices that promoted communication and helped prevent misunderstandings.

A variety of functional patterns for improving relationships between R & D centers and laboratories and their field users were examined. When we attempted to describe and categorize those linking strategies, it was obvious that many techniques overlap. There are no neatly packaged tactics for educational researchers to use in developing field relationships; the strategy depends upon the nature of the research and the unique needs of the field users. However, one or more of the following procedures may have high payoff for both sides.

An Exchange System

The simplest system linking centers and laboratories to the field is the exchange or barter strategy. Products, research results, problem solutions, or money are exchanged for field time, use of sample populations, or money. This "consumer" concept has the advantage of being a clear-cut and balanced transaction in which both sides gain. An additional positive aspect is that an exchange relationship is easily understood by both parties because analogues in business and industry have provided successful, long-term models.

But there is no Better Business Bureau for the users of educational research products, and buyers on both sides need to beware. In this particular barter situation the value of the products (results, information) is difficult to assess, and the seller may not be providing what is really needed. For example, twenty hours of personal interviews with teachers may be perceived as more valuable than a two-page analysis that took twenty hours to write. An added disadvantage of the exchange system is that researchers often spend inordinate amounts of effort and time cultivating a market for services that may not be really mutually beneficial.

Using individuals or groups to do research on a consultancy basis is an exchange strategy that can set the stage for furthering research interests beyond solving immediate school problems. Whether the researcher-consultant is hired by a district, or field users are paid as consultants to researchers, the relationships are usually well defined and formalized contractually. The research network could benefit by encouraging more educational personnel from the field to act as paid consultants to the centers and laboratories. This "reverse consulting" has many advantages—bringing in practical expertise, marshaling field support, and solidifying future contacts in the field.

Research networks have used many variations of exchange strategies to relate to field users, and reactions and responses to the results were also varied. "Our research staff has become a sales force" was one viewpoint expressed, while others felt "the research was valuable to everyone concerned." In any event, if the linking tactics are specific and tailored to each unique field situation, exchange strategies can be effective.

Political Influence

Essentially a selling process without a product, political influence is a strategy that may have to be used before an exchange relationship can be developed. Successful political strategies can have great potential in the educational change process by building a supportive field network based on trust or political trade-offs. For example, the Stanford center first gained approval of the Environment Program's proposed survey research project from the Association of California School Administrators. The association, in turn, then sent letters expressing confidence in the study and encouraging Bay Area school districts to participate. On the other hand, researchers who are inept politicians may find themselves spending their limited time and money at political fence mending with no guarantee of productive outcomes. As a result, some research organizations keep away from influence tactics and retreat into their world of pure research, saying, "We'll leave the pork-barreling up to Washington."

Somewhere in limbo—neither a political influence strategy nor a total immersion as participants in the research effort—is the use of advisory boards and committees. As a political maneuver, teachers, administrators, and community members have too often been used as tokens of field involvement in the planning and implementation of educational innovations. This criticism does not mean that advisory boards can never function as a limited form of political influence or participation strategy. One successful example is the Stanford center's use of teachers from diverse programs and organizations to provide valuable inputs to research. In addition, a superintendent of a local school district serves as a voting member of the center's executive board. These examples point out the potentialities of advisory committees as vital contacts with field users that may lead to the deeper involvement of participation.

Participation

This linking strategy supports programmatic, nonlinear research by providing constant feedback from the field users who share a personal stake in the outcome. Participatory relationships mean that field users and R & D organizations together define common problems, plan the research and development procedures, specify tasks, implement ideas, and evaluate results. The participants' status should be based on the expertise each brings to bear on the shared problem. Certainly it is time for professionals in the field who provide their insight and practical experience to be awarded the respect of their peers in research. Working together on common tasks not only results in research focused on real problems, but also has the advantage of breaking down the myths which kept researchers apart from teachers and schools.

Of course, participation can be unwieldy, time consuming, and difficult to coordinate—speed and efficiency are not outstanding features of the democratic process. But despite the conflicts inherent in two such different perspectives as those held by research organizations and school systems, the benefits of participation to both may surmount the difficulties.

Consortia

The consortium is a group of organizations that pool their existing sources of money, time, and knowledge in attacking common problems. The Participation to Activate Change Today consortium, organized by the Wisconsin R & D Center, is an impressive example of a successful, integrated consortium formed to implement the multiunit school concept. All of Wisconsin's multiunit schools (more than 300) are involved; six schools of education run training programs; liaison committees operate at many large school districts; installation teams visit consortium members with problems; and state coordinators are trained by the center. Naturally this system requires a heavy commitment from the center for staffing, financing, and coordination. Although the basic organizational structure of the consortium is often unstable, and the size creates difficulties in coordination, the advantages may outweigh the logistic disadvantages.

One variation of the consortium strategy was the regional cooperative, as developed by the Appalachia Educational Laboratory. The mountain districts of the region were too small and too limited in resources to implement educational innovations. As a solution to this problem, superintendents, teachers, and administrators shared knowledge, equipment, and methodology on a regional basis. The districts furnished the personnel and funds, and the laboratory avoided a directive role. The laboratory, on the other hand, accumulated data on school problems and operations, enabling it to push forward in research.

Still another type of consortium linked the Southwest Educational Development Laboratory in Austin, Texas, with the Dallas Public Schools, the Perot Foundation, and the Texas State Department of Instruction. These cooperating agencies agreed to implement a variety of educational innovations at one location. This *site* development strategy contrasts sharply with the *product* development strategy that stresses a single product for use in a number of settings. The laboratory is an equal partner, neither dominant nor directive, and gains much by its dynamic relationships with the other organizations.

Demonstration

In one sense, demonstration techniques are methods to sell research ideas to potential field users, but demonstration models can also be described as efforts by researchers to create their own field users so that others can judge the applicability of the research. A long-standing prototype is the laboratory school, a ready-made experimental site where pilot projects are highly visible applications of theoretical research. Special summer schools can provide a short-term intensive workshop for research implementation; another possibility is for research and development organizations to contract for an entire district of field users, running long-term, well-articulated programs. Whatever the scope of a demonstration strategy, "pure" researchers and theoreticians may find pilot projects a comfortable entry into the practical world of educational problems.

It is necessary, though, for demonstration projects to include ways for schools to adapt ideas to their own use. One criticism from teacher-observers has been, "Those concepts work beautifully in the controlled laboratory school projects, but we want to know how to apply the ideas to our own schools." There is also the danger of creating prototypes that are too expensive to be used on any large scale by school systems.

Research Vouchers

One possible linking procedure is a *voucher plan* giving field users federally funded vouchers exchangeable for R and D time, staff, or products. The concept, untested at the research level, is being tried in pupil selection of elementary schools, and the assumed advantages in that area may prove true in the research context: (a) a "free market" with users determining needs; (b) reducing the influence of university-based centers by encouraging competition—and possibly higher quality—as researchers vie for money; and (c) built-in long-term evaluation—if the center performs well, it will get future contracts; if not, the user looks elsewhere.

Of course, educational vouchers may not be a panacea either, for they could negatively affect long-term basic research and development capabilities, as researchers chase after the immediate payoff of voucher money. In addition, the flow of educational fads could undermine the development of a stable pool of talented researchers. In any event, a voucher strategy deserves to be examined.

Although this discussion of tactics for linking research efforts to field users by no means exhausts the possibilities, the strategies presented do merit trial. As long as both researchers and school personnel jointly choose a method of cooperation that best suits their needs, and as long as they keep the lines of communication open, the strategies and the results may be effective.

Facilitating Field Relationships

Whatever the strategy chosen to involve research and development institutions with their field users, establishing definite management procedures will facilitate the relationships. Effective management techniques include formalizing arrangements between organizations; specifying their financial agreements; balancing the staffs of centers and laboratories; developing policies regarding feedback; and promoting interaction with educational training institutions.

Formalizing Field Arrangements

As we investigated this issue we found that arrangements between research centers and field users ranged from contacts with a minimum of formality to agreements that ensured the recognition of rights and responsibilities on both sides. Formalized approaches worked well because expectations were understood, commitments were clear, financial resources were accounted for, and feedback to the schools was sustained. Conversely, simple verbal approval and vague letters subjected research centers to later criticisms on the grounds of unspecified or misunderstood purposes and nonexistent follow-up.

An example of successful facilitative management practices was found at Southwest Regional Laboratory (Los Angeles), where field-testing was done only after a detailed agreement had been approved by both parties. Only specified laboratory personnel contacted the schools directly, their purposes and procedures were approved by school administrators in advance, and full reports were given to districts upon completion. This prevented the familiar complaints from school personnel that researchers used schools without benefiting the district.

As a result of Southwest Laboratory's careful, detailed procedures, a number of school districts requested that they be used for field-testing and research purposes. In contrast, people at centers using informal approaches often discussed the difficulties of getting into districts to do research. These observations reinforce the recommendation that relations between R and D organizations and field users should have at least a minimal degree of formality, with clear, written statements of intent and responsibility, and regularized systems of feeding information back to the host schools.

Financing Field Activities

We found many different patterns of payment for field activities. In some cases school districts paid R and D organizations for services as they tested new products; the laboratory in Austin derived much of its budget from this source. Other R and D organizations did the opposite, paying the host school or district to allow them to work there; this was done by the Johns Hopkins Center for Social Organization of Schools and by Pittsburgh's Learning R and D Center, which contributed over $100,000 per year to Oakleaf and Frick schools, where its innovations were tested.

Another financial arrangement was payment by a third party—a private foundation, a federal government agency, or the state department of instruction—for the trial use of innovations. Research for Better Schools (Philadelphia), Wisconsin, and Southwest Laboratory provided examples of this pattern.

Whatever the financial patterns adopted, they must be designed to fit each center or laboratory and the districts they use, and must be tailored to meet available funds. We therefore recommend no specific type of funding, but urge that information be distributed to make all concerned parties aware of the various possible financial arrangements. In addition, federal officials in NIE should review financing for field-testing efforts so that their budgets reflect an appropriate emphasis on such activities.

Staffing R and D Organizations

The staffing pattern undergirds the basic philosophy of any research and development effort, for at the nerve center of every organization are the personnel who translate visions into action and who use organizational structures to accomplish goals. Because this paper argues for increased involvement of R and D organizations with field users, staffing patterns are a crucial issue and bear reexamination.

The research and development system is an excellent place for the birth of coherent new disciplines of applied social science, with their own norms, reward system, and methodologies. One such role developed by a number of laboratories and centers is the "educational catalyst," a person remaining in the field to test and implement R and D programs, and to act as a liaison with the R and D organization. CEMREL had such "change agents" in Chattanooga, Nashville, Bowling Green, and the Pennsylvania Department of Instruction. The National Laboratory for Higher Education instituted the "Educational Development Officer"—a full-time staff position devoted to systematic organizational change in colleges, using innovations from R and D research. The Center for Urban Education in New York used full-time, on-site field personnel in its Community Learning Centers to implement innovations and provide feedback.

Another emerging profession in research and development is the "linking" role that involves the complex task of moving new concepts, procedures, materials, or structures from research into everyday educational usage. The linking role can be *managerial,* joining research and practice; *developmental,* subjecting the results of basic research to the test of practical use; or *implementary*, translating research material into operational procedures. All these linking roles demand creative skills, serious training, and methodological tools equal to those needed in basic research. Inherent in the liaison position of the linking professional or field relations specialist is the problem of serving two masters, a problem which exposes those who fill that marginal position to criticism from both directions. Therefore, the linking staff should be afforded the prestige, money, and influence comparable to that of the research staff.

Along with the evolution of new roles and disciplines, R and D organizations should consider broadening the social science base of their staffs to include such existing disciplines as sociology, anthropology, political science, and history. Creating interdisciplinary mixes of personnel not only brings a multifaceted approach to problem solving, but also expands the narrow range of disciplinary concerns traditionally limited to psychology and education. In fact, our research into the disciplinary backgrounds of key R and D personnel shows that the largest number, both with Ph.D. degrees (38 percent) and without (43 percent), are in education. Among the professional employees in the social sciences there is dominance of psychology backgrounds (with Ph.D.s, 19 percent; without Ph.D.s, 41 percent). This disciplinary imbalance may have limited the R and D vision—the problems identified, the methodologies used, and the conclusions arrived at. Another staffing matter concerns part-time versus full-time staff and faculty status versus nonfaculty status. University-based R and D centers typically employ as part-time associates faculty members who undertake multiple research and teaching commitments and who appear more interested in disciplinary, theoretical inputs to basic research. Since development is as important and as difficult as basic research, R and D centers must simultaneously solve two problems—recruiting academic researchers who will not divert the center from developmental goals, and employing skilled nonfaculty personnel, giving them the necessary status and incentives.

Many different solutions to the staffing problems have been successfully applied. In the centers at Oregon and UCLA, for example, some faculty members participated in research and development on almost a full-time basis. At the Wisconsin center nonfaculty professionals with the title of "scientist" directed the development

work. The R and D Center for Teacher Education at the University
of Texas (Austin) employed strong nonfaculty personnel in a highly
systematized operation. The Pittsburgh center is notable for the
quality of its work and also for its heavy nonfaculty to faculty ratio,
averaging about six to one; this approach mixed strong faculty input
for conceptualization and research with high-status nonfaculty professionals concerned with practical problems and field issues.

Who staffs the centers and laboratories and how their expertise is
used are paramount to the successful impact of research on field
users.

Developing Feedback Policies

In order to maintain goodwill and to provide an objective evaluation of ongoing programs or innovations for professionals, responsible
feedback must be given regularly. Over the years critics of educational
research have felt the lack of usable feedback so strongly that they
appear ready to tell researchers to return to their ivory towers.

An example of potentially effective guidelines for feedback are
these proposed by a faculty committee of the Stanford School of
Education:

1. Before a project starts the project staff should carefully plan
and budget for responsible feedback on the progress of the activity.

2. The host agency should be given specific details about proposed
feedback, its timing, and its nature.

3. Issues of coauthorship and appropriate credit in writing from a
project should be settled formally and in advance.

4. When a project is well under way it is helpful to have a preliminary feedback session. This sustains morale in the project and
uncovers troublesome issues early.

5. When an activity is completed it is important to report to the
field users. The written feedback document could be supplemented
with a public presentation of the project.

Whether these particular guidelines are adopted is not important;
what is crucial to field personnel is that follow-through be explicit
and maintained.

Promoting Interaction with Education Personnel Training Institutions

Changes in education cannot occur without first reaching those
whose direct impact on students is greatest—teachers and school

administrators. Although nearly every person connected with education goes through a formal training program in colleges and universities, our studies concluded that there were very few effective relationships between the R and D network and the personnel training network. The studies isolated only small-scale interactions, such as Wisconsin's use of six schools of education to train personnel for the multiunit schools, Austin's connection with a number of teachers' colleges, and Stanford's skeletal involvement in a teacher education program. Despite the widespread circulation of R and D activity reports to an audience which includes educational professionals, the channel between teacher education and the R and D network is predominantly one directional. To prepare future school personnel for active participation in R and D work, research centers and laboratories should expand their interactions with schools of education.

Some types of innovations from the R and D centers and laboratories seem natural inputs to schools of education: new teacher training programs, new methods of institutional evaluation, proposals for reworking administrative structures, and new curriculum packages. In addition, teacher training institutions are the most logical places to develop and educate students for the new research-practice linking professions.

Guba and Clark view the problem of linking research with practice somewhat differently. They seek to construct a conceptual system to guide planning for the utilization of relevant knowledge:[2]

The general thesis of this paper can be stated simply:

a. The current federal policies and programs for educational knowledge production and utilization (KPU) are inadequate either to build a base of political support for educational R and D or to effect a significant improvement-oriented change in educational practice.

b. The inadequacies cannot be accounted for or explained away on the basis of conditions (political or structural) that have arisen in the past two to three years. In fact, they are embedded in the conceptual view of educational KPU that has come to dominate the field. This perspective, a unified-systems view, presupposes and/or attempts to effect a linked set of productive agents and agencies, each of which assumes discrete responsibility for a segment of Research-Development-Diffusion-Adoption effort to achieve a commonly agreed upon goal of ultimate KPU productivity.

c. This view has set in motion a cycle of failure in educational KPU productivity by:

1. Establishing unachievable aspirations.

2. Ignoring the idiosyncratic (idiographic) goals of individuals and individual agencies in the educational KPU community.

3. Changing policy and program directions persistently and frequently in an attempt to overcome failures in program achievement provoked by conditions one and two above.

4. Overcentralizing and overcontrolling programs which have been assessed as failures.

d. Retention of the current unified-system view of educational KPU will defeat the field's effort to mount an adequate federal KPU program in education which can command broad-based support within and outside the profession. To achieve this goal, there must be a reformulation of the conceptual structure on which the program is built that is:

1. Complete—sufficient to account for the full spectrum of KPU functions.

2. Balanced—responsive to both individual (idiographic) and institutional (nomothetic) goals of the wide spectrum of agents and agencies involved in educational KPU.

3. Realistic—reflecting with fidelity the real world of educational KPU.

A Brief Historical Perspective

The current unified-system view of educational KPU is the culmination of twenty years of federal involvement in educational R and D. Federal programs in this field, beyond the social bookkeeping function, began with passage of P.L. 531 (the Cooperative Research Act) in 1954. The Cooperative Research Program adopted a predominantly *social science* perspective of the field, that is, the identification and support of productive research scholars in the framework of an open competitive project mode modeled after other federal efforts in the National Institutes of Health, the National Science Foundation, and the Office of Naval Research. This approach soon came under attack on two counts: that it was *incomplete,* ignoring development, diffusion, and adoption in favor of exclusive attention to research; and that it was *unbalanced,* concentrating entirely on idiosyncratic individual efforts which resulted in non-cumulative, nonprogrammatic inquiries.

In response to those criticisms, two new views were introduced in rapid historical succession: the *substantive* view, intended to achieve more distinct problem focus, as exemplified in such efforts as Project English and Project Social Studies, R and D centers in vocational and special education, and the Right to Read program; and the RDDA view, intended to flesh out the spectrum of KPU functions and agencies as exemplified by the Educational Resources Information Center, Title III of the Elementary and Secondary Education Act of 1965, and the research training provisions of ESEA, Title IV.

These efforts did redress the lack of completeness fairly well, and made significant gains in terms of balance. So reinforced, it required but a small conceptual leap from these views to the notion that a system could be engineered in which component agents and agencies had defined roles linked together in such a way that the output of one component agency, for example, the R and D center, would become the input for the next agency, for instance, the development activities of the regional laboratory. Such a unified system would, of course, have shared goals which could be achieved by ensuring productive output at the adoption end of the RDDA continuum. The inexorable trend of the past twenty years has been toward the establishment of just such a national system of educational KPU. As a matter of fact, in establishing NIE, Congress charged that agency with responsibility "to build an effective educational R and D system" as one of its four major objectives.

A Current Assessment

This era of movement from the social science perspective to a unified-system view has not been without progress. Most importantly, it broadened the programs of the field across the spectrum of RDDA activities to agency settings which had previously been nonexistent (for example, education laboratories) or ignored (for example, local education agencies). But despite such gains on the dimension of completeness, the federal involvement in KPU seems to be deteriorating at an alarming rate. Support in Congress appears weaker than it has been in twenty years—NIE has just experienced two budget reductions in consecutive fiscal years. Equally as alarming, political support within the profession for appropriations for educational

R and D is at best weak. And it is extremely difficult to demonstrate that "the system" is producing what it purported would be produced, that is, a consistent flow of inventions being adopted by schools as solutions to their operating problems.

These conditions, it can be argued, are true at least partially because the systems view overcorrected for the idiographic *imbalance* of the earlier views and failed dismally on another, equally important criterion whose importance became apparent only when some experience with the systems approach had accumulated, *realism,* the extent to which the conceptual view reflects with fidelity the real status of the individuals and agencies that comprise the KPU arena.

Balance is achieved not simply by introducing a missing element, but by achieving a state of harmony among elements. In attempting to redress overemphasis on the idiographic dimension of educational R and D, the new programs allowed support for individual researchers to almost disappear between 1965 and 1972. This year, the Field Initiated Studies Program of NIE is spending less money on the research of individual inquires than CRP spent in 1962. Worse yet, as the programs become nonfield initiated they become federally initiated and controlled through such devices as "Requests for Proposals" for performing federal procurement directives. In attempting to avoid programs that were idiographic, nonaggregative, and inefficient, the systems perspective has tended to produce KPU effort that is centralized, narrow, and unimaginative.

The perspective can be faulted equally on its lack of realism: the idea of a unified system for educational KPU simply does not make sense in terms of what is "out there" to systematize. There is certainly not a commonly agreed upon system output for KPU among state and local agencies, education laboratories, colleges and universities, and private R and D project institutes. Much to a designer's consternation, such agencies do not and will not assume predefined roles in KPU. Education agencies are almost overwhelmingly not primarily KPU producers, that is, their primary output is the teaching act. They are unlikely to redesign their organizations so that they can be linked for KPU purposes.

A New Perspective

The KPU planner, it may be asserted, would be much closer to descriptive reality were one to picture an educational KPU *community* rather than a KPU system. One would, for example, note that since few hierarchical relationships with corresponding authority allocations exist among the agencies and agents of educational KPU, terminology might be better borrowed from community analysis, for example, "political" and "negotiation" rather than "allocation" and "authority." Or that terms like "delegation" or "assignment," congruent with a system metaphor, are more likely to be portrayed accurately by the term "persuasion"; or "responsibility" by "commitment." The concept of "community" is a heuristic metaphor to bring to bear in understanding the American educational KPU enterprise.

Literally, of course, the KPU establishment is *not* a community, so that slavish adherence to the idea of community as a *model* might easily lead to conclusions which would fail on the criterion of reality. To circumvent this possibility, the new perspective to be proposed will be referred to not as a community view but as a *configurational* view, although the root metaphor of community as a suggestive and illuminating concept should continue to be borne in mind. The first point to be made, then, is that:

The configurational view is roughly analogous to the concept of a community. The variety of institutions and individuals concerned with and functioning in educational KPU are more likely to consider themselves to be related to one another in a community sense than an organizational one.

The term "configurational" was chosen to describe the view adjectivally because it (1) connotes a conformation of elements that exist in a definable territory; (2) assumes that the elements are (a) specifiable, and (b) relevant to one another; and (3) implies that the interaction of the parts is more than the sum of the parts, as, for example, configurationism in Gestalt psychology. The term also implies that there is no direct analogue available which can simply be chosen and used as a model for this particular configuration of organizations as they relate to one another in terms of KPU. From an operational point of view, the term configurational may be interpreted to mean that:

The educational KPU domain or territory can be defined as the full range of operating educational agencies or institutions in the country. They can be inventoried or specified both individually and in various groupings. Their relationships to one another are generated usually by their attention to a function other than KPU, that is, training. They are, however, related in varying ways to KPU functions and do, or at least could, maintain a productive interaction to attain a comprehensive, shared social goal, that is, improvement-oriented change in education.

Brief definition is simpler than brief portrayal of the configurational view. To attempt to provide a feel for the perspective, brief answers to three basic questions that can be raised about any perspective dealing with educational KPU will be offered:

1. What are the goals and functions of educational KPU as established by the configurational view? Like the unified-system view, the configurational view is cognizant of and endeavors to account for the full range of KPU functions. However grouped, and with no assumptions of linear flow, KPU needs to attend to the functions of generating new knowledge; inventing, engineering, and testing solutions to operating problems in schools; disseminating knowledge and solutions throughout the community; and adapting, adopting, and institutionalizing solutions to operating problems in educational units.

In broad terms the configurational view accepts the goal for educational KPU that has been propounded in one form or another in federal policy for a century, that is, the goal of educational KPU is improvement-oriented change in educational operations. However, since this overall goal has appeared to be acceptable in the context of *any* perspective of educational KPU, it is obviously too general in form to be operationally useful. Perhaps the question, in the final analysis, is less a "goals" question in relation to KPU than a goals question in relation to the institutions populating the domain. With very few exceptions, such as education laboratories and centers, private research organizations, and a handful of graduate institutes for the study of education, education institutions are not primarily KPU production organizations. This is not to say, obviously, that they are not concerned about, or are not active participants in, KPU, but rather that their line function is operating the American school system, and their dominant activity is educating students or supervising that education. For such institutions, KPU is a handmaiden function—a route to improvement or a form of social action.

The essential goal-level rethinking required by the configurational view is reflected in this phenomenon of goal orientation of the organizations and institutions in the educational KPU domain. Sensible, effective national policy will assume that educational KPU is a form of social action for the members of the educational community; will recognize that most members of the community will accord educational KPU only second-level priority, and then most likely for idiosyncratic purposes; and will view these idiosyncratic goals for KPU as opportunities to be seized upon in policy formation rather than as obstacles to be overcome in the achievement of homogenized national goals for educational KPU.

2. *What organizations and individuals populate the configuration?*

The configurational view assumes that the educational KPU community encompasses the full range of diverse institutions and individuals involved in the social process field of education. This means that:

The total population in the community is very large and differentiated.

The individuals and agencies group themselves together for purposes and functions which are not related primarily to KPU.

Agencies and individuals are represented in the community simultaneously across many levels and characteristics so that no generic classification is adequate to reflect their interests, activities, or goals; for example, a large city school district may have more in common with an education laboratory in KPU policy considerations than with a rural school district; a classroom teacher may feel legitimately that the local professional association is a better representative of the school district than, for example, the school board.

The interest of the organizations and the individuals in the configuration in joining together to support the concept of a community will be determined by the comprehensiveness with which the population is considered in educational KPU policy. Currently, most of the population assumes that they are the invisible or less visible segments of this society.

3. *How do the organizations and individuals in the configuration work in and relate to educational KPU?*

The constituent agencies in the configuration may be characterized as follows:

Not sharing a common conception of necessary or desirable KPU outputs.

Viewing KPU activity as subordinate to their primary activity.

Functioning essentially independently of one another.

Playing overlapping roles in relation to KPU.

Maintaining no binding authority relationship to one another.

Operating with no function flow across organizational boundaries.

Sharing minimal activity relationships.

Thus, the KPU community is described, in the configurational view, as highly decentralized, consisting of a number of more or less independent and coequal members, who may from time to time find it helpful to form temporary alliances but who, in the main, retain their independence, shun authority and activity relationships, and engage in as many different kinds of KPU activities as seem to be needed and feasible for them to maintain their self-sufficiency.

In view of the preceding characteristics, the configurational view suggests that the social science view was overly decentralized while the unified-system view has become far too centralized. The configurational view searches for a middle (transactional) state of organizational balance. While it recognizes the need to attend to general goals of educational KPU which transcend the aspirations and goals of individuals and individual organizations and agencies, it also suggests that the achievement of these goals, at least in part, is a sine qua non of the attainment of broader national goals.

It is the assertion of this paper that the configurational view performs significantly better on the criteria of completeness, balance, and realism than any predecessor view which has characterized the educational KPU enterprise in this country. In relation to completeness, concern for this criterion was built in at the level of an undergirding assumption; moreover, the perspective takes explicit account of the fact that constituent KPU community members have different goals that relate to KPU only secondarily. In relation to balance, the configurational view takes a transactional posture, holding that there must be elements present in any federal KPU plan responsive to both individual and programmatic interests and that there must be sufficient flexibility to allow some "play" back and forth between these two positions as circumstances permit or demand. Finally, in relation to realism, the configurational view displays a willingness to take the world of educational KPU on its own terms, and to work from that vantage point to generate policies and programs, rather than to construct a model that makes untenable assumptions about how things ought to be.

Epilogue

Rooted in what appeared to be strong rational-logical under-pinnings, the unified-system view of educational KPU has been employed extensively in federal planning for KPU programs for a decade. Its apparently unassailable rational base, however, does not stand the light of empirical or experiential examination. That is not the way the world is.

The key question becomes whether or not adoption of an in-adequate perspective makes any difference in planning. Surely it does, and it has. Just as the limitations of the social science view were holding back development in the field, so the inaccuracies of the unified-system view have provoked breakdowns, hostilities, and failures in educational KPU. It would be foolish to contend that the mercurial history of federal-level KPU efforts over the past decade is all attributable to any single cause. Societal disillusionment is not restricted to educational KPU, but the unified-system approach to educational KPU has contributed to this general situation by holding out unrealistic performance expectations as a modus operandi.

The conceptual structure supporting federal policy in educational KPU has itself contributed directly to the expectation shortfall of KPU programs and agencies across the country by holding out un-reasonable expectations for sequential productivity and linkage among the involved producing agencies. The evaluative questions being posed by federal planners are based on assumptions that act as if a world existed which simply does not exist. The evaluations, subsequently, are negative: the predictable next step is the invention of yet another substitute program intended to restructure the world as it "should be" which, in turn, simply introduces further conflict and failure.

A first step in breaking the current negative cycle has thus been suggested. Like it or not, a more realistic conceptual view of educational KPU must be presented to, and acted upon, by those who decide upon national KPU policy. Unless the extant structure of the field is taken into account, and unless the legitimate interests of the individuals and agencies that populate the domain of educational

KPU are honored, there will be no significant progress in the development of long-range, effective policies for educational KPU. For it
is only by building a strong constituency of such individuals and
agencies that new directions can be charted and successfully followed.
Such a constituency can emerge and flourish only to the extent to
which there exists a conception of educational KPU to which all can
subscribe.

*Proposals for developing closer linkages between researchers and practitioners
are worth considering because each group can contribute to the activities of the
other. Neither production of knowledge nor putting it into practice would,
however, be advanced by an effort to direct research solely to the problems
recognized as critical at any particular time or to seek guidance for the improvement of educational practice only from the output of any and all contemporary research organizations. In many cases, ineffectual practices are not
recognized or have not been analyzed. The identification and analysis of particular
problems are important steps that do not depend heavily on new research. They
should be based on knowledge accumulated over many years as well as techniques
of observation and data collection about which the advice and assistance of
researchers can be helpful. The design of a system to improve educational
practice is the task of developers and practitioners more than researchers.
Implementation in schools and colleges is not so much a matter of gaining
acceptance of some device by teachers as it is the development on the part
of teachers of a more adequate understanding of the phenomena with which
they deal and providing assistance where necessary in devising new ways of
working with students, that reflect this understanding. An emphasis on teachers'
(and administrators') understanding and participation in problem solving is not
inconsistent with the views on linkages presented above. It does, however, give
more attention to the middleman. In R and D activities in industry, the middleman is commonly an engineer. He is neither a researcher in the strict sense nor a
practitioner. In educational R and D there has not been a clear definition of the
role of the middleman nor even an identification of him as such. In the workshops, first instituted in the Eight-Year Study of the 1930s, the middlemen were
members of the curriculum and evaluation staff. Most recently, some schools
have appointed coordinators to work with teachers in Title I programs. They
help to identify the problems of learning encountered by particular "disadvantaged" children, and they assist teachers in devising a system for improving
the learning of these children. Knowledge is sought by these coordinators from
all sources known to them. In that sense, they are links in the KPU chain.*

*The future of educational research and development will be influenced by
the extent to which schools and colleges recognize that their improvement will
not come mainly from adopting some idea or device that is given wide publicity*

for a moment. A more effective procedure is to maintain a system of monitoring programs so as to identify problems as they arise. Then the practitioners themselves will need to be involved in seeking and testing solutions, drawing directly or through middlemen upon relevant knowledge to guide the development of possible solutions.

Notes

1. J. Victor Baldridge *et al., Improving Relations between R & D Organizations and Schools* (Stanford, Calif.: Stanford University, 1973), 10-21.

2. Egon G. Guba and David L. Clark, "The Configurational Perspective: A New View of Educational Knowledge Production and Utilization," *Educational Researcher* 4 (April 1975): 6-9.

7. ALTERNATIVE FUTURES

Predicting the future of a social institution is hazardous, and if the prediction is relatively precise it is almost certain to be wrong. Kenneth Boulding remarked at a conference on the future shape of schooling: "There is one thing we can say with great confidence about the future. It will be full of surprises."[1] This chapter presents several alternative views about the future of educational research and development. The reader may find one more plausible than the others, or he may use the views outlined here to suggest the general range within which future developments can be expected.

The vision of the future expressed most often by scholars in other fields foresees modest prospects for educational research and development. In this view, basic research will represent from 10 to 15 percent of research and evaluation activities. The public generally, it is argued, accepts the claim for the value of increasing knowledge, even when it has no immediate utility, as long as the cost of producing such knowledge is a very minor part of public budgets. When I was chairman of the Research Advisory Council of the Office of Education I found this attitude reflected in both the legislative and executive branches of the government. Large increases in federal support for educational research and development were responses to Sputnik and later to the aspirations of the Great Society, in which research and development would guide the way for the war on poverty and the elimination of social discrimination and injustice. When these expectations were not quickly realized the public attitude, and the government's attitude, toward research changed. Expectations that had been overly optimistic dropped to a level that underestimated the social contributions of research.

In this modest view of the future, 85 to 90 percent of funds for research and development provided by public sources will be directed to applied research and to evaluation. These activities will largely be responses to public concerns, such as the improvement of education for disadvantaged children and the development of a functional system of occupational education appropriate for a modern postindustrial society. The amount of money spent on research and evaluation, according to this vision, will grow no faster than the gross national product. In 1975 the amount provided for educational research and development by all agencies of the federal government was approximately $200,000,000.

This view of the future does not expect basic research organizations to be closely linked to the operations of schools and colleges. Many studies will be conducted in cooperation with schools, but no attempt will be made to assist practitioners with their immediate problems. On the other hand, a variety of disciplines will be involved in educational research; thus many of the studies will be interdisciplinary in nature.

Applied research and evaluation activities will be closely linked with ongoing school and college programs. Operational research and action research will represent a major portion of these activities. Their support will be obtained largely from state and local budgets with partial support from federal funds. Money available for applied research and evaluation will fluctuate with the changing patterns of public concerns.

Educational development of products will continue to be largely in the hands of firms that provide supplies and equipment, particularly educational publishers, with guidance and assistance from teachers and professors. The development of systems of teaching and learning will, in the main, be done by professors in schools and colleges of education, cooperating with classroom teachers. Some public and other nonprofit agencies, however, will carry on educational development for two chief purposes: to provide new programs and devices for learners whose needs are so specialized that they do not constitute a profitable market; and to serve as a pacemaker and yardstick against which the performance of private firms can be judged.

Such a modest picture envisions training programs for research and development that approximate those suggested in Chapter 5. With a population growth near zero, quality of training rather than quantity can be emphasized, and opportunities for internships can be developed more fully. Since young men and women quickly respond to information about the changing job market, it is expected that the apparent oversupply of persons trained for research work will disappear, and enrollments in graduate school will more closely reflect job opportunities. This is the modest projection of the future.

The view of the prospects for educational research and development in the immediate future presented by the leadership of the National Institute of Education is one that is less modest and more centralized. The NIE Task Force on Resources Planning announced initial plans for carrying out its legislatively mandated responsibility to "build an effective educational research and development system."[2] The following are the major sections of that report, as recounted in The Educational Researcher:[3]

The plans are organized into efforts designed to build (1) internal NIE capability to monitor the R and D system and operating system of education, (2) the R and D system, (3) the linkage and support system, (4) capacity in the operating system, and (5) field-initiated research on the processes of educational change. The chapters on the second and third programs, which are most directly pertinent to the mandate underlying the plans, are reproduced here in full text.

Building the R and D System

Problem

The past decade of growth in education knowledge production and utilization has witnessed the creation of new R and D institutions, the introduction of rapidly increasing numbers of new technologies, and a new role for the federal government as both a major initiator and sponsor of education R and D. However, that system is still in its infancy. R and D models often borrowed from the "hard sciences" have not always been appropriate to the solution of complex social problems. New models more closely related to the requirements of social research must be invented. The new institutions and functions have yet to become part of an interrelated and mutually supportive endeavor. Present financing arrangements leave the viability of some new institutions in doubt. At the same time, the appropriate role of market forces and nonmarket interventions is unclear. Scientific communities which seem so vital to the growth of knowledge in other fields are still weak and fragmented. Strategies for increasing the responsiveness of R and D performers to the client's needs are underdeveloped.

Objectives

The objectives for a program to build the R and D system can be described as follows:

To achieve greater understanding of the structure and functions of the education R and D system, including the identification of factors contributing to the productivity of the system.

To strengthen the infrastructure of institutions, personnel, and technology for conducting education R and D.

To improve NIE management of R and D.

To strengthen the interface between the research and development systems and systems for linkage and utilization.

Strategies

Because we have a very limited knowledge base from which to work, the conduct of further policy studies and research is essential to formulating long-range intervention strategies. The monitoring function described earlier is a major feature of this set of activities.

In addition to long-term research and analysis, we also propose a series of special studies aimed at particular issues which we regard as crucial to NIE. These issues should be addressed in the near future, prior to the initiation of the comprehensive data collection strategies embodied in the monitoring system. A long-range program of policy studies and research would focus on the following areas:

The internal operations of the knowledge production system. The studies will examine the manner in which various government policies influence system development and would describe and analyze the current status of the three subsystems:

The institutional subsystem of performers: what they do, how they do it, and how well.

The personnel subsystem: including nature, distribution, and competence of personnel and the influence of training, selection, and recruitment strategies.

The special facilities subsystem.

The dynamics of the system's interaction with the client groups. The studies will examine the relationships of the school's market structure to the producers of R and D and the incentives in the R and D system for being responsive to the problems faced by schools.

R and D systems in fields other than education and the education R and D sector in other countries. The studies will compare the nature, operations, and effectiveness of other systems with those of the U.S. education R and D system.

NIE management strategies. The studies will identify alternative planning, procurement, monitoring, and evaluation strategies; assess their implications for attracting to NIE high-quality research and development; and propose new management strategies.

All of these studies are designed to gain a better appreciation of the dynamics of the knowledge production and utilization system and the problems which affect its ability to facilitate improvements in the nation's schools. These endeavors will identify new intervention strategies for improving system operations and for assessing the effects of proposed interventions on the total education enterprise.

The following short-term projects are proposed for the near future.

POLICY STUDIES AND RESEARCH

1. *Policy analysis of the roles and problems of nonprofit and university contractors.* With the transition of the educational laboratory and R and D center program to NIE, a major shift in policy from "institutional support" to "program purchase" was made, severing the special relationship between the government and these institutions. It is time to assess the policy's effect on these institutions. More generally, it is time to consider the impact of government procurement policies on universities and other nonprofit organizations, and to identify other factors affecting the productivity and viability of these organizations. Key issues would include:

What has been the effect of the program purchase policy on the effectiveness and viability of the laboratories and centers?

Does the nonprofit sector need strengthening, or is it viable and effective under present arrangements?

What policy should NIE have on management fees?

What is the effect of the copyright policy in providing independent research funds or contributions to the capital structure, and is it contributing to and encouraging the dissemination of products in an optimal way?

The utility of this project depends on securing the effort of experts who have studied these issues—possibly in fields outside of education R and D—to assess available information, supplemented by limited field visits to some of these institutions. The expected product would be a series of short-range policy recommendations for an NIE procurement policy and the identification of key issues for more intensive study.

2. *Policy study of alternative methods of increasing minority participation in education* R and D . . . . For the past ten years

education of minority groups and the disadvantaged has been one dominant target of education R and D. This concern is now embodied in the legislative charter of NIE. R and D personnel who are themselves members of minority groups can be expected to have insights into these problems not available to others, and minority groups are still generally underrepresented in the R and D work force. As it is not clear what strategies would best alleviate this problem, a policy study is proposed to assess the various options.

3. *Study of incentives affecting career decisions of R and D personnel.* From a strictly supply and demand point of view, there is no reason to believe that education R and D should not be able to attract the quality and mix of persons needed for effective work. Yet it would appear that education R and D continues to be a low-prestige field not attractive to our best talent. Clearly, more definitive data are needed to confirm these impressions. We need to know more about the incentives and motivations affecting the career decisions of scientists and technicians, with particular reference to structural elements of the system which might be altered to improve the field's attractiveness and holding power. We propose to initiate a project to design and pretest such a study.

STRENGTHENING INSTITUTIONS, TECHNOLOGY, AND PERSONNEL

1. *Workshop on research management.* R and D on a scale sufficiently large to require sophisticated management techniques is relatively new to education, but clearly the present situation requires such skill and technologies. The sponsorship of a workshop on research management would signal NIE interest in this field, provide support for the growth of a related scientific community, improve the skill of personnel employed in management positions, and add to the technological base.

2. *Workshop and seminar series on problems in evaluation methodology.* Evaluation has emerged as a key specialty contributing to the conduct of R and D in education and other social problem fields. Evaluation research is important to policy analysis, formative evaluation is essential to product development, and summative evaluation provides product validation data needed by clients and consumers in order to make rational adoption decisions. Pure forms of experimental design are rarely feasible, and new designs and methodologies are needed to cope with the complexities of the

problems and the vagaries of working in ongoing social institutions. This project would sponsor a series of workshops and seminars on evaluation methodology with objectives comparable to those for the workshop on research management, that is, to signal NIE interest in the field, provide support for the growth of a scientific community, improve the skills of personnel working in evaluation, and add to the technological base.

Building the Linkage and Support System

The rapid growth of education knowledge production has not been accompanied by a parallel surge of educational reform. There seem to be many reasons for the apparently limited impact of education R and D. One problem is certainly related to the nature and quality of R and D products. The previous section suggests some ways to begin increasing the quality of the system's outputs. There are other problems, however, which may be responsive to strategies we can more rapidly initiate. These are generally related to difficulties which confront the operating system. For example, school staff:

Has trouble in locating and using information which is relevant to its needs and which is in an understandable form.

Has trouble selecting between vast numbers of R and D products which seem undifferentiated in terms of effects.

Needs to have access to a wide variety of alternative solutions to particular problems.

Has trouble implementing and sustaining new educational approaches which are often unfamiliar and sometimes perceived as threatening.

One strategy to alleviate these problems may be to develop a much more comprehensive and interactive system, linking together the producers and consumers of education knowledge and products and providing professional support to the operating system. We have previously discussed several organizations and strategies which now carry out the linking and support functions. These included publishers, ERIC, state departments of education, and teacher centers. There are many others. We propose here three initial program strategies designed to understand, improve, and strengthen this system. They are:

An Information Dissemination Strategy

A Consumer Information Strategy.

A Product Delivery Strategy.

Recommendations related to external linkages are also contained in the chapter "Building Capacity in the Operating System." Taken together, the several strategies relating to linking mechanisms proposed in this report are intended to provide a knowledge base that will eventually permit governmental units at the local, state, and national levels to build together a network of linking mechanisms uniquely adapted to the needs of education.

Consumer Information

Education decision makers, chief state school officers, legislators, school boards, superintendents, parents, principals, teachers, and children all determine the content and style of education in our schools. Often, they must make important decisions without much information about the possible effects of the various alternatives. Customarily, most evaluation reports have concentrated on the degree to which a particular product or program produces the desired outcomes for the target population. Occasionally they have commented on unintended effects as well. Only rarely have they included other information that has a direct bearing on the decision to adopt and the process of implementation—information as to community reaction, financial costs of implementation, organizational consequences, effects on classroom discipline and vandalism, anecdotal accounts of how schools and teachers have coped with those problems, and so on. Yet this kind of information is often more important to those who must adopt and implement the product than are data on target group outcomes. Not only is information of this kind generally unavailable about government-sponsored programs, it is very rarely generated for innovations developed in the operating system. State education agencies, among others, are increasingly interested in disseminating information about good practice but have often lacked the resources and methodology to determine the value of innovations developed in the schools beyond intuitive grounds.

Objectives

What is needed is a program of consumer information to provide:
Better means to *identify and test* promising practices.
Better *verification* of product evaluation procedures and results.

More and better *information* on product performance and the process of adoption and implementation.

Alternative strategies for providing this information in an *appropriate format* to consumers.

Strategies

In order for the Consumer Information Program to provide useful and credible information to its intended audiences it must:

Stimulate improved evaluations of NIE-sponsored programs and products which generate reliable information about the effectiveness of alternatives, essential conditions for their implementation, and limits of their adaptability to local constraints.

Identify promising products and practices generated by the operating system as well as by R and D sponsors other than NIE, and develop a procedure for collecting and verifying similiar consumer information.

Experiment with a variety of ways to effectively communicate consumer information to interested client groups.

We propose to initiate the following experimental programs:

1. *A product verification unit* will be established in the Office of R and D Resources. This unit will collate and review information about NIE products, and verify the evaluation procedures used. This would include verifying the presentation of information related to adoption and implementation. Appropriate courses of action will also be identified to verify non-NIE-sponsored programs and products.

2. *A conference of state agency personnel, evaluation specialists, government representatives,* and others will be held to identify means of producing consumer information about promising school practices. The results of the conference will be used to develop a cooperative program with state agencies and others to identify and verify school-based practices, to be implemented in future years.

3. *A product format study* will be initiated to determine how to format information about promising products and practices so that it is useful to consumers. A contract will be let in fiscal 1974 to empirically assess the relative merits of different content and presentation styles for educators and school boards.

4. *A catalogue of NIE-sponsored and verified products* will be developed in fiscal 1974 based upon initial results of the product format study described above. This catalogue will be designed to

facilitate the selection and implementation of alternative products. In the future, similar catalogues should be produced at least on an annual basis, and should include non-NIE products and school-based programs. In future years, other methods of communicating such information will also be attempted.

5. *A program of research and evaluation* will be carried out in future years to improve the knowledge base upon which consumer activities rest and to determine if the program is achieving its objectives.

The Information Dissemination and Communication Program

PROBLEM

The foregoing analysis indicates that externally generated knowledge is a major resource in the process of educational reform. The results of research shape future research, direct the development of new educational solutions, and provide new insights into operating educational problems. The experience of one school district which has designed or implemented an innovation can simplify the task of another school district in adapting or implementing a similar solution to its own problems.

To varying degrees, members of the educational community have access to a substantial number of information resources. Some of these are focused on specific groups of clientele, such as professional associations and their journals, and others may deal with specific educational problems, such as the network of over 400 special education instructional materials centers. One, the Educational Resources Information Center (ERIC), has undertaken—with only partial success—to provide the full educational community access to the comprehensive body of documentary English literature about education. An earlier portion of this document has given a brief description of the largest information storage and retrieval systems in the world. It is, of course, operated with funds from the National Institute of Education.

Both because of ERIC's scope and its NIE sponsorship, any NIE plan for improved access to educational information must take into account its strengths and weaknesses. Hundreds of thousands of uses are made of ERIC resources by educators every year, yet its users make up only a fraction of the educational community. If one takes the perspective of a potential user of an information service, the reasons for underutilization of educational information become apparent.

From the user's perspective, there are four major requirements of a responsive, serviceable information system:

Comprehensiveness: few educators (or performers in other fields, for that matter) have the time or inclination to seek information from several sources prior to making a decision or undertaking a course of action.

Relevance: the information provided must be germane to the needs of the user. If one is seeking empirical evidence, he should not receive speculative papers; if one is interested in descriptions of practices in the school, he should not receive reports of laboratory experiments.

Utility: the information should be as directly usable as possible; it should be compatible with the current skills and knowledge of the user.

Accessibility: the user should be able to have preliminary access to the information system locally, and preferably in his own work setting; the response to the information request should be timely for the user.

From this perspective, neither ERIC nor any other educational information system, nor all of them together, are meeting the needs of the educational community. However, even if all these requirements are met, the information system will not be acceptable unless its costs are reasonable to the user, to the system operators, and to its sponsors.

OBJECTIVE

The objective of the Information Dissemination and Communication Program can be inferred from the preceding discussion; namely, to provide timely access to all relevant and useful knowledge relating to education for the diverse members of the educational community, including teachers, administrators, school board members and other policy makers, researchers, and developers.

STRATEGIES

Attainment of the objective requires an information system which performs the following functions in a cost-effective manner:

Acquisition of all relevant documents and other knowledge relating to education;

Screening the acquired information for authenticity, relevance, and utility;

Indexing the acquired information so that individuals addressing the information system may readily identify needed and relevant information;

Storage of information in a manner to facilitate . . . ;

Retrieval of required information by system users in a timely and economical manner;

Dissemination of information in forms required by the user including print, microform, computer tape, interpersonal communication;

User Services for ready and timely access to the system and assistance in fully exploiting the system;

Development Information Products such as bibliographies, state of the art papers, and interpretations and syntheses of knowledge on significant educational topics, tailored to key user groups.

For any system to perform these functions appreciably better than existing services, it will be necessary to design and implement it over a period of several years. All of these functions are being performed to a greater or lesser degree by ERIC at the present time, and their performance is essential in providing information to educators while a newer, more viable system is emerging. We shall, therefore:

1. Initially maintain the ERIC system, making such improvements as are possible with our current knowledge about the requirements of education and the state of the art in information science and technology.

2. Initiate necessary experiments, economic studies, and policy analyses which will provide specifications for a more viable and responsive information system.

3. Design, incrementally, necessary major modifications or alternatives to the emerging information system. Our initial efforts, both in short-term ERIC modifications and longer-range system designs will center around four improvements:

Scope of Information Covered. We shall determine whether the currently available knowledge in ERIC should be broadened or narrowed, examining the feasibility of providing either physical access or references to such information as data files, instructional materials, and school-based information.

Improved System Access. Beginning with attention to the list of functions above, we shall determine whether other functions are required, and whether some of those listed can be left to the attention of other instrumentalities. It will also be necessary to determine the types of location of performers of these functions and the possibility of cooperative use of local, state, and federal resources in maintaining the system developed.

Transformation of Information into Usable Forms. An expanded program for generation of problem-oriented information products will be begun immediately and further expanded in future years.

4. Field-test, adapt, and implement design alternatives for the improved educational information system.

Two activities intended to provide immediate improvement will be initiated at once:

User Study. Support will be provided for a series of activities intended to identify current satisfaction, dissatisfaction, and information-using styles of individuals in various roles in the educational community. These user studies should provide an initial basis for making decisions about changing the coverage of literature and other educational information. In addition, they will provide the basis for initial plans for modification of local user services.

Information Transformation. NIE is currently in the process of identifying high-priority topics on which interpretations and distillation of knowledge into more usable forms are required. Among the sources used are feedback of stated user needs from extant information service centers and the results of a survey of information requirements supported in preceding years. Using these data and staff analyses, NIE will issue requests for proposals for state-of-the-art papers and other information products on high-priority topics.

Three other activities will be initiated during the current fiscal year or early in fiscal 1975, contingent upon the availability of funds:

Economic Analysis of ERIC. This study will address the issues of costs, markets, and the utility of the current system. A cost allocation model will be developed to examine the costs of each system component. The market analysis will answer such questions as: the degree to which demand for products and services depends upon price structure, the degree to which an information system can be self-supporting, and the effectiveness of marketing techniques in increasing the user population. These data will be used in future policy decisions and system design.

User Services. Awards will be made to operating information centers to design or implement improved or expanded information services to user groups. In one case, this may be little more than providing referral services to sources of technical assistance; in still others, an operating information service center may be supported in providing its services to a contiguous area which does not now have such services. In still another case, a center might be supported in the design of broader and more responsive information services.

Continued Experimentation with On-Line Computer Retrieval. Experience to date suggests that on-line, interactive computer search capability permits more rapid retrieval and generally higher user satisfaction with the results of a search of the ERIC file. Further experimentation with these techniques, both to improve their utilization and to explore means of reducing their cost, will be undertaken.

The objective of this program is addressed to serving the manifold needs of a variety of different groups in education, each having differing areas of expertise and each operating under a different set of constraints. This requires that the ultimate configuration of an effective educational information system have a wide range of products and services, tailored carefully to the diverse requirements of the various client groups.

Whatever may be the inadequacies of the current ERIC system for researchers, developers, and graduate students, they have the capacity to make use of the system (that is, access to the products of the system and skill in reading and interpreting the results of research) and some level of incentive to seek out and use information products. Most individuals in the operating sector, be they policy makers, executives, or teachers, have relatively less capacity to seek out and exploit the products of an information system whose collection consist largely of research reports.

We believe, therefore, that the primary, but not exclusive, focus of our initial efforts should be to enhance the utility of ERIC and whatever system grows out of it for the educational practice and decision-making community. Every effort will be made, however, to ensure that these efforts will concurrently serve the interests of the scholarly community.

These few initial activities will permit some immediate upgrading of the responsiveness of ERIC. In addition, however, they will provide the basis for a preliminary design for an improved and expanded information dissemination system.

Delivery of Development Products

Improving educational practice is dependent in part upon the existence of a wide variety of program and product alternatives, generated by both the R and D system and the operating system, which decision makers can select, adapt, and implement at an acceptable cost with reasonable assurance of effectiveness.

However, a variety of problems with current mechanisms for delivering R and D products to the operating system limits their accessibility and, consequently, their utilization. These include a lack of continuity and articulation between developers and publishers, problems with products with low-profit potential, problems of coordinating technical assistance with product delivery, lack of market forecasting, lack of knowledge about the costs and benefits of different dissemination strategies, and lack of incentives for developers and publishers to promote widespread effective utilization of their products and to revise material in the light of implementation effects.

OBJECTIVES

A series of strategies will be developed to improve education's product delivery system by:

Increasing our understanding of the relative effects of a variety of dissemination strategies.

Increasing the continuity between product development and dissemination.

Experimenting with a variety of incentives for improving the delivery of high-quality R and D products.

STRATEGIES

We propose to initiate the following experimental activities:

1. *A managed copyright program.* NIE should devise a series of experimental strategies to: manage the incentives and rewards NIE makes available to developers-distributors; and demonstrate, create or, in rare instances, subsidize markets for NIE-sponsored products. This would include:

Demonstrating the existence of a market before inviting distributors to handle the product.

Where a market cannot be demonstrated, NIE should create an initial market before inviting distributors to handle the product.

When an initial market can neither be demonstrated nor created,

NIE should consider the possibility of subsidizing the limited distribu-tion of products which may meet uniquely important needs.

This program would include other experimental strategies to: provide incentives and rewards for cooperative arrangements between agencies that specialize either in development or in distribution; provide incentives and rewards for agencies to extend their internal capacity to handle the full array of functions from product develop-ment to broad-scale distribution; and vary royalty sharing and royalty rates in contracts with developers-distributors in exchange for ex-pansion of such services as evaluation and training.

If these strategies were to be implemented both by the National Institute of Education and by the balance of the educational research and development community, and if continuing progress toward the objectives is achieved, the prospects for the future include a greatly expanded program and one that is much more systematized than either the present one or that indicated by the modest picture presented previously. It is a different alternative future. It more nearly represents the outlook of the Bureau of Research of the United States Office of Education as reflected in a report to the Organization for Economic Cooperation and Development (OECD) prepared in 1969 by Hendrik Gideonse, director of Program Planning and Evaluation for the bureau. In the final para-graphs of that report Gideonse wrote:

Regarding educational research, several consistent judgments and conclusions emerge across the reviews and evaluations. The need to adopt a more forthright posture regarding the support of basic science relating to education is present, balanced by the equally strongly stated need to focus educational research, and particularly development, on the solution of high-priority problems.

. . . A third continuing concern is aimed at the present quality of the entire research and development enterprise in education. Calls for closer ties to the parent disciplines and the involvement of more individuals of high repute from the social and behavioral sciences emerge with regularity.

A fourth continuing thread can be found in the judgment that educational research and development is clearly undersupported financially and in great need of more forceful, and more directed, manpower development policies. Also, the importance of the rela-tionship of research programs to the research and education com-munities finds expression in the concerns evinced over review and planning procedures, advisory mechanisms, the politics of research, and "vertical and horizontal" integration.[4]

The National Institute of Education is working on the implementation of the kind of future outlined in the planning document cited above. A good illustration is the attack it is mounting on the problem of reading and language skills, as described in the following report appearing in American Education.[5] *The report outlines the several research efforts that are planned, but does not present in any detail how the research activities are to be related to developmental ones and to the practitioners in America's decentralized school system. This may be a major problem area that will determine the future of the NIE, as it has for the Office of Education's earlier research programs.*

The National Institute of Education has set up a new program to ensure that children develop the "essential skills"—language and reading competencies and mathematics and social skills—they need to become full participants in society. The Essential Skills Program became part of NIE's Office of Research last December, when the National Council on Educational Research—NIE's policy-making body—designated essential skills research as one of the institute's five priority areas. The program is directed by Marshall Smith, associate professor of education and social policy at Harvard and a Visiting Scholar at NIE. Smith and other Essential Skills researchers are working to find ways for educators to provide every American with the skills demanded by today's society.

Planning for this work began last summer, when NIE sponsored a study group on verbal communication to recommend an institute program of research and development addressing all aspects of language communication—reading, writing, listening, and speaking. The group, chaired by George A. Miller of Rockefeller University and composed of experts from other universities and federally funded projects, compiled the extensive "Report of the Study Group on Linguistic Communication," which included specific recommendations for NIE's research into reading.

According to that report, a substantial portion of the U.S. population does not read well enough to function in society:

Some 12,000,000 people fourteen years of age and older cannot read as well as the average fourth grader, yet seventh-grade reading ability is required to perform such skilled or semiskilled jobs as machinist or cook.

Approximately 60 percent of the nation's thirteen-year-olds cannot follow directions in a relatively simple cookbook.

An estimated 18,000,000 adults cannot read well enough to file applications for Medicaid, Social Security, bank loans, or drivers' licenses.

Not surprisingly, a disproportionate number of poor and minority people are counted among those who have difficulty with even the simplest reading tasks. Those who fail to acquire the language skills that society demands are, as a consequence of this lack, often deprived of the information that is necessary for them to exercise their full rights of choice as citizens. They have difficulty reading voting literature, telephone directories, employment brochures, product labels, and other consumer information.

NIE's study group on communication also found that little is being done to help these people. Its report reads in part:

When we ask what is being done for those who have passed through [the] instructional system without acquiring basic literacy, the answer seems to be, "very little." When we ask what research is receiving support, most of it seems to be directed toward the established practices of the traditional system of reading instruction. When we ask what is being done to match reading instruction to the cultural background of the student, we find many small, interesting experiments in progress, but no national program. When we ask what is being done to teach reading-as-understanding, no one seems to know how it should be done.

The Essential Skills Program, after considering the recommendation of the study group, established two major goals for the reading and language component of the essential skills work. First, NIE will attempt to improve the probability that all children—especially the perceptually handicapped and bilingual or those who speak a dialect of English—acquire the basic literacy skill of "decoding" or mastering letter-sound correspondences. Second, NIE will try to make it easier for all children to meet the demands for reading comprehension encountered in grades four to eight.

Projects designed to meet these goals are already under way at NIE, some having been transferred to the institute last year from the Office of Education, and some having been awarded funds through NIE's research grants competition in fiscal year 1973. Others are being designed by the staff of the Essential Skills task force.

Projects relating to the first objective—helping children to acquire basic literacy skills—are for the most part basic research studies to discover how the learning process works in many different environments. The projects explore the specific processes and abilities involved in acquiring linguistic skills. For example, studies are being made of the complex process of decoding, in which a child must recognize the shapes, arrangements, and groups of letters; move his or her eyes with precision and control; and produce sounds in response to visual clues. According to the linguistic study group, "The wonder is not that some children fail to master [this process], but that most children succeed." This process must be understood so that reading can be taught in the most reasonable manner possible.

Projects dealing with this problem include studies of the relationship between the development of reading skills and cerebral dominance in the left hemisphere of the brain, work toward developing a model of the process of word recognition in children, and analyses of the results of children's preferences for using sounds or pictures in a learning situation. In addition the Essential Skills group will soon launch a major project designed to improve methods for recording eye movements and analyzing their relationship to the ability to read.

Other basic literacy projects are concerned with understanding the important factors—both in the school environment and in outside life—that affect the development of language skills in young children. These factors might include behavior associated with effective and ineffective teaching, classroom structure, open classrooms, summer vacation, and teachers' speech patterns. The Individually Guided Education Program of the University of Wisconsin, for example, is studying the effects of an alternative instruction system on the achievement and motivation of elementary students. The students receive individual instruction from teachers and are part of a flexible school organization based on student ability rather than on artificial grade levels.

The NIE researchers are also intent upon identifying and understanding factors outside the school environment that affect linguistic development. The study group's report states: "Literacy skills are not developed solely in the classroom—the problem is not just the child and the teacher. We should broaden our outlook to include special problems of minorities, adults, understanding processes, types of reading materials, and variables outside the classroom."

Since NIE's mandate is to help achieve a national policy of

providing an equal opportunity for all children to receive a quality education, the researchers are especially concerned about "the need to better connect what the child brings to the first grade and what the first grade presents to him." Many projects are concerned with the effects of home environment on children and with the special problems of the bilingual or bidialectic child. For example, Erica McClure of the University of Illinois is investigating the process by which children raised in a bicultural setting acquire two languages. Clark Williams of Missouri Southern State College is analyzing American Indian and Chicano responses on standard tests to identify those that are free from cultural bias. And the Intercultural Reading and Language Development Program at the Northwest Regional Education Laboratory is trying to increase the reading abilities of American Indians, Alaskan natives, Samoans, and economically disadvantaged children in grades one and two by using teaching materials that involve people, places, and experiences that are familiar to the children.

Less is known about the processes involved in understanding and interpreting reading material than is known about the development of basic literacy skills. Therefore, a major effort in the Essential Skills Program in the next few months will be directed toward its second priority: increasing comprehension skills in grades four to eight.

A few research grants projects explore this question, and the task force will spend some time synthesizing knowledge from these and other programs already under way—the Office of Education's Right to Read Program, for example. Smith is also planning a computer simulation project that will develop a model of the processes of comprehension in reading and listening.

More Essential Skills projects will begin soon. Approximately $1,000,000 of the program's money will be allocated in NIE's fiscal year 1974 research grants program. Smith estimates that this money will be allocated to about twenty Essential Skills projects in the field. This year, 695 researchers applied for funds, and special consideration is being given to projects that focus on students from low-income or minority families. Planning for a program concerned with the development of mathematics skills will begin next November.

The main goal of the Essential Skills Program for this year, according to Smith, is to map a long-term research agenda in reading and language that includes specific objectives and plans. The agenda will draw upon syntheses of what is known in the area of reading and language and upon new ideas to be generated this summer.

A study conference has already been scheduled for specialists in the field of reading and language—researchers, administrators, and teachers. Their goal will be to come up with a tightly related set of perhaps 100 to 200 specific research projects which promise to increase understanding of reading and language development, after which NIE will issue requests for research proposals addressing the specific problems identified in the conference. This strategy is expected to enhance cooperation among Essential Skills professionals, as well as to produce new knowledge.

The federal investment in reading research and development has up to now been small and dispersed among many agencies, each of which funded projects consistent with its own mission. NIE is the only federal agency, other than the Department of Defense, that has the authority to commit its funds to many different types of reading projects, from basic research studies, to developmental programs, to program evaluations. The agency is, therefore, in a favorable position to coordinate the fragmented information that is being produced on reading in such a way that the efforts of federal programs to understand the processes of reading development are as effective as possible.

A third alternative future for educational research and development in the United States was that presented to President Johnson by his Educational Task Force of 1964. This report was prepared at a time when the Cooperative Research Program of the Office of Education was authorized to support educational research projects and programs and also research and development centers in universities. The report viewed educational research projects and programs as similar to research activities in other academic fields, adding gradually to our fund of knowledge about the educational enterprise. It recommended immediate substantial increases for these activities after which funding would increase in proportion to the general increase in federal support of schools and colleges. The research and development centers were seen as institutions capable of conducting interdisciplinary as well as multidisciplinary research on major educational processes and problems. It was expected that each center would concentrate its work in different problem areas, using sufficient funds to include the development of systems and devices as well as being able to concentrate "a critical mass" to make intensive studies. Recommendations were made for great and immediate increases in support for these centers, followed by a plateau of expenditure as the centers tested their viability. With the demise of those that were not viable, it was expected that new ones might emerge while the viable ones obtained greater support should that be necessary.

The task force proposed the establishment of new institutions called education laboratories. Their functions were not to be primarily research or development. They were designed, rather, to assist schools and colleges in identifying and analyzing their serious problems and in bringing together the available knowledge and experience to guide practitioners in their attack on those problems. It is unfortunate that the legislation in the Elementary and Secondary Education Act of 1965, which authorized the support of education laboratories, did not sufficiently specify the intent of the task force. Thus, many of the laboratories operated more like research and development centers than as middlemen helping practitioners attack problems through use of knowledge and collective experience. It is possible now, however, to imagine a future in which such middlemen play an institutional role in the research and development enterprise.

The 1964 Educational Task Force of 1964 also suggested the establishment and development of supplementary educational centers. The report recognized that much of what children and youth learn is acquired in out-of-school experiences. But many of the informal educational institutions, like the home, the job, and the church, are having less opportunity to furnish constructive learning experiences than in earlier days. At the same time, parks, museums, libraries, youth organizations, service institutions, and the like have great potential for providing constructive learning experiences for children and youth. The task force recommended that the federal government encourage the study of these possibilities, the designing of educational experiences with the cooperation of the institutions involved, and the utilization of these supplementary educational centers by the schools. This area of educational research and development has been implemented more fully by those interested in community schools than by others. It is a conceivable development in an alternative future, and it was an integral part of the recommendation of the task force.

A final illustration of an alternative future is presented in an article in a British journal by a scholar at the Institute of Education of the University of London. The article not only provides the reader with a sense of what leaders of educational research in England are discussing, but it makes an unusually comprehensive statement on many of the issues touched earlier in this volume.[6]

Educational research workers are frequently criticized for the "irrelevance" or merely marginal relevance of their work. It is said that the problems they tackle are not those of the class teacher, nor have they solved central and burning questions on what makes children learn or the best ways of organizing a school. What is more, it is alleged, the findings of elaborate inquiries are either confirmations of "common sense" or manifestly absurd—that is, they merely prove what we think we know, or, failing to confirm our prejudices, must be rejected.

In remarks of this and similar kinds there is a grain of truth, and sometimes more. Much of what is listed as research in education and in the sciences basic to education has been conducted principally for the purpose of gaining a higher degree. University regulations and the natural tendency to play safe have led students rather to choose the intensive, usually statistical, study of a small area than to attempt the solution of highly complex problems. The language of research reporting—especially in a thesis—is hedged about with qualifications which fail to satisfy the practitioner's thirst for striking and certain generalizations. A few leaders in the field have managed to direct and coordinate thesis work of their postgraduate students over a very long period and have emerged with a coherent study of a considerable series of related problems. Godfrey Thompson in Edinburgh in the field of psychometrics; Burt in London in the study of delinquency, backwardness, and the theory of ability; Valentine in Birmingham pursuing the psychology of early childhood, and, at the same time, fostering an extensive series of studies of adolescence; and Schonell, over a lifetime, studying the teaching of arithmetic, reading, spelling, and written English and embodying the results in a widely used series of textbooks—these and others are the giants of the dawn of the educational sciences in this country. Neither must we forget the immense American, French, Swiss, and, recently, Swedish contributions—and particularly the work of men such as Thorndike, Stanley Hall, Terman, Piaget, Vallon, and Binet.

Of course they have not provided all the answers to all the questions posed by teachers; they have not done more than lay the foundations of theory in some parts of the field. We could hardly expect more since the experimental study of education is barely seventy years old. But since the turn of the century we have gained at least as much knowledge of the educational process as was won about disease from the time Harvey expounded his theory of the circulation of the blood (1616) to the rise of notions about environmental sanitation in the nineteenth century.

In fact, one can reasonably claim that the contributions of research to the development of education cannot be passed off as slight or marginal—they are certainly far in excess of what might have been expected from the insignificant financial resources devoted to it. We know more about education, about children, about the social psychology of the school, about learning and its hindrances, about how to measure the educational product, and such like matters, than we as yet apply in practice. And such knowledge as we have has been at least as central to the educational revolution which has taken place since 1918 as have driving impulses of economic or political and social kinds.

The fact that the general body of teachers has to be reminded of these and similar facts is significant. It suggests that teacher training has been somewhat at fault if the profession is not critically aware of the scientific bases of much of what it does. One paradoxical result of this is that now, in a climate suddenly favorable to technology and scientific advance, many professional educators are hard put to it to distinguish between reasonably firmly based theories from which good educational experiment may be derived, and bodies of doctrine which may be called pseudoscientific since they owe as much to particular social or political philosophies as they do to objectively ascertained fact.

Research in education, emerging rapidly from the "tintack and glue" era, is now confronted with immense opportunities. The last four years have seen a proportionately huge increase in the money available for educational research and an even greater increase in the funds directed toward curriculum development. In 1958, the total expenditure on educational research was of the order of £150,000 annually, representing no more than .01 percent of the total expenditure on education. The figure for the current year certainly exceeds £500,000—still a fraction of 1 percent of the total educational expenditure, but nonetheless a massive advance. In addition, private foundations have given funds for curriculum development, and the Schools Council has been set up for much the same purpose. We may expect too, that the Social Science Research Council, and particularly its Educational Research Committee, will stimulate considerable research activity in the sciences basic to education and in specifically educational research.

Money, and the public interest which it represents, is of vital importance, but it is not everything, and may present considerable dangers. Because of the comparative neglect of education as a research field, there are few organizations in this country at present capable of sustaining major programs over the minimum period of years necessary to gain worthwhile results. Men and women with the basic scientific qualifications as well as educational experience—particularly firsthand experience of the classroom—are few in number and hard to come by. In spite of the general advances in psychology, child development, psychometrics, social psychology, statistical methods, and sociology in the past decade, we have little but partial theories directly relevant to education. Finally, there is a noticeable (and understandable) tendency on the part of some teachers and administrators to consider the process of research to be too slow and to wish to plunge on their hunches without too much in the way of objective checks on their value. With education and educational decision making moving more and more into the center of political and social controversy, voices are not wanting to play upon this, to promise quicker results from hastily mounted impressionistic studies and to urge particular reforms as if they were already justified by research evidence and merely needed implementation.

Such strains and tensions are inherent in rapid growth, but they may prejudice the sound development of research in education—which is after all the biggest and probably the most fundamental field of applied social science—and of education itself. In the future, then, we must get our ideas straight, and sort out the relations between the sciences basic to education and direct educational research activity, and between research and curriculum or other development and general decision making in education.

It is perhaps easiest to work backward in thinking about this. Let us imagine a primary school teacher in the relatively common, apparently simple situation of wishing to choose between teaching arithmetic of a traditional kind of traditional means and teaching the so-called "new" mathematics. How can research aid him? He would probably like to know how far either form of mathematics conformed to the general structure and development of children's thought—and here, such basic theory of child development as exists and bears upon this problem would help, insofar as he was able to interpret and apply it to individual children. He would also like to know—since both approaches might be equally possible—in what ways the outcomes, both short- and long-term, differ from each other and from one kind of child to another. He would also probably wish to know how far the goals achieved by either method were compatible with others he wanted to achieve in the education of his pupils. Thus, the teacher will be using his professional knowledge and skills to interpret and use information and basic theory from the social sciences and from the technology of his craft. He will attempt as a result to set up some viable hypotheses. He will also quickly realize, if he approaches his work in a critical objective spirit, that these hypotheses should be tested (and the outcomes of the work measured) in real day-to-day situations—that is, he or someone else on his behalf will have to undertake some action research. When all this is finished, he will arrive at a conclusion such as the following: that method or curriculum A appears to achieve effectively results C, D, and E, while method B produces results X, Y, and Z, and that result M is common to both. His previous study of theory and his more or less elaborate action research will not have solved his problem for him in any absolute way. But they will have defined the possibilities of his alternative curricula, suggested refinements of technique, sharpened up and made clear the choice to be made. The choice itself between attainable goals, the value judgments about the aims of what he does, he will have to make on moral, philosophic, social, or perhaps even political grounds.[7]

A similar situation arises in deciding on matters of policy at the national or local level—to stream or not to stream; whether transition from primary to secondary schooling should take place at eleven, twelve, or thirteen; whether to teach a foreign language to young children. There is no objective way of making the final *value* judgment. Research can define the limits within which choice is possible and avoid the confusion between the desirable and the practicable which befogs so much educational controversy. It can also provide the means of seeing whether the aims proposed by the innovator or policy maker are achieved. In short, while it cannot tell us, for example, if it is *good* to set up comprehensive schools, it can throw light on whether the proposed aims (or others) are achieved, which forms of organization are more or less efficient than others in achieving them, how far the gains under one system are greater than, different from, or simply incompatible with, those of another.

These examples throw light upon the relations between the growth of knowledge in the basic sciences (psychology, sociology, child development, and social psychology) and the applied, essentially multidisciplinary, science of educational research, and between both of these and what is called "development." Research in education is essentially concerned with the problems of learning as they confront the teacher, the administrator, and the policy maker in all the complexity and untidiness of the real day-to-day situation. It is an applied science—or rather an array of investigatory techniques— derived from the social sciences. It is therefore dependent upon theoretical and experimental developments in the various contributory fields, both for its hypothetical structures and its research instrumentation. It is, too, the bridge between the "purity" of academic research in, say, child development, learning theory, or even animal behavior and the teacher in front of his class. Just as the academic research worker supports by his work the technology of educational research, it is from the practitioner that the educational research worker derives his problems, and through him that he checks his hypotheses.

The relation between research and development is only a special feature of this broad pattern. Anyone who wishes to build a new curriculum in, say, English, will normally wish to acquaint himself with basic research work on language, on the growth in children of verbal linguistic concepts, with general learning theory, and so on. He will also attempt to set up some practical (and, one would hope, definable) goals which he wishes to achieve; and he will study both the results of any controlled experiments in teaching English and the experience of his colleagues. The result of all this should be something more than hunch; it should be the clothing of some reasonably founded hypotheses in a detailed program of work, of materials, and of teaching method, and a statement of his objectives in clear operational terms. In effect the initial stages of development should arise from a dialogue between the specialist teacher of English, dedicated to certain beliefs and value assumptions about his subject, and the more factual objective body of knowledge about language and about children. From them should come a synthesis which the developer believes to be *good* and practicable. When he puts his experimental curriculum into practice he is taking up a position. He believes that what he is doing is beneficial, more beneficial than anything so far achieved. He is committed. At this point, the educational research worker should be called in to evaluate objectively, and in a detached way, the innovation proposed. His questions will be of two kinds. Does the innovation achieve its stated goals? Does it achieve (or inhibit) any others? The object of evaluation thus is to draw up, as it were, a profit and loss account in the narrow context of the particular innovation and, equally importantly, in the broader context of the whole educational process. If this evaluation is undertaken by the developer himself, it is difficult for him to avoid prejudice in favor of his own value judgment, and still more so, to look beyond the confines of his cherished specialty to the wider general framework of education. Moreover, it is rare for the specialist in a given subject to command the array of techniques—psychometric, statistical, psychological—essential to adequate evaluation. Without some such impartial weighing of practicability, comparative achievement, educational profit and loss, there is considerable danger that striking innovations will lead to serious educational confusion; at best we shall remain the victims of educational fashions which hitherto have changed from decade to decade without notable advance.

Having said this, it is fair to add two qualifying remarks. The first is that adequate evaluation is an expensive, complex, and lengthy process, not to be lightly undertaken. The second is that some at least of its complexity and cost is due to the inadequacy of our investigatory instruments, and their relative clumsiness. We are suffering from the lack of investment in the past in educational research and in the social sciences generally—a situation which we may hope to remedy, albeit slowly.

Closely allied to specific evaluative studies are the survey and operational researches which have been—mainly for financial reasons—the main examples so far of large-scale research in education. The Scottish *Mental Surveys*,[8] the National Surveys[9] of 1955 conducted by the NFER, and the Ministry of Education Reading Surveys[10] are examples of the operational researches, and have produced a rich harvest of facts about broad categories of children, about the general levels of ability and achievement and the relationships of these to socioeconomic factors and different forms of educational organization. Among other things, these surveys, with the work of Jean Floud,[11] Douglas,[12] and others, and the study of the workings of allocation methods at the threshold of secondary education[13] have done a great deal to call in question notions of "innate" intelligence, to throw light on the genuineness of fashionable concepts of equality of educational opportunity, and to define in some detail the way in which the problems confronting teachers vary according to the kind of place and the kind of school in which they teach.

Many matters can best be studied by international surveys. Of these to date, the most sophisticated in design and widest in scope is the IEA study of the outcomes of mathematical education.[14] Because it has been conducted in the educational systems of a dozen countries of varying socioeconomic backgrounds, widely different cultural and educational attitudes, differing levels of investment in education, and types of school organization, it permits us to distinguish whether such broad factors as age of entry to school are or are not significant in terms of educational output, whether (and how) differing degrees of selectiveness affect the distribution of mathematical skills in the population, and even to answer the question, "Does more mean worse?" It also allows us to gain some notion of how far and with what overall results the "new mathematics" is spreading in the schools, and whether the alleged superiority of direct grant and public schools is a function of their quality as schools or is due to an initially superior intake.

In these and similar surveys there is a large element of what we might call "operational research." Changes have been made and innovations introduced, the effects of which it is possible to pick up at the time of a survey. If, however, we wish to get nearer to the heart of the educational process than we can by a "snapshot" technique, we have to attempt a related series of observations over a considerable period. This occurred on a broad front and with relatively simple means in the study by Douglas mentioned earlier.[15] More specific questions relating to the reading, to the careers and fate of individual children, to the interaction between children, teachers, aspects of school organization and of classroom climate are answered by such work as that conducted over ten years by Dr. J. M. Morris for the NFER.[16] Taking schools, textbooks and methods as they were in daily life, this study concerned itself with the relative effectiveness of different teaching methods and combinations of method over a long period of children's lives and, in the light of detailed and repeated observations in the classroom, has done something to disentangle the relationships among method, materials, teaching skill, and the qualities the child himself brings to his learning.

Other studies of a similar kind—for example those of Dr. Goodacre—
have concerned themselves with a detailed examination on the one
hand of teachers' attitudes and knowledge of the early stages of
reading, and on the other of the social background of their pupils
and its bearing upon readiness to read.[17]

Surveys and operational research studies tend to be based on
large samples and group measurement techniques, largely because
the effects they are seeking to describe can only be established
certainly when sufficient numbers of pupils are involved to ran-
domize fortuitous differences. Moreover, when resources are small,
the research worker is faced with the often agonizing choice between
establishing normative facts firmly by using large numbers of children,
and the more sensitive detailed study of numbers so small that he
cannot be sure of the significance of any findings he may achieve.

As our armory of hypotheses and of investigatory techniques
improves, and as trained workers and money become more readily
available, we can hope to get the best of both worlds in what might
be called "action research." In this approach, changes based upon an
amalgam of theory and practice are deliberately introduced, and are
varied systematically and in fairly massive ways. In the curriculum
and method field, the current long-term study of the introduction of
French in primary schools[18] is one example. The work on teaching
methods and materials for primary school mathematics[19] is another.
Rather narrower and more precise in scope is the work on the initial
teaching alphabet.[20] The Swedish researches on comprehensive education, in which schools of a comprehensive type were set up in one-
half of the city of Stockholm, and their working studied over a
period of years in comparison with more selective schools in the other
half, illustrate the kind of action study which enables organizational
reform or change to proceed with reasonable caution and objectivity
in understanding, modifying, and evaluating what is done.[21]

Probably a large part of the future of what is specifically *educational* research lies in the development and refinement of action
studies of all kinds—in the field of curriculum, in specifically
pedagogical methods, in differing ways of deploying teaching and
other staff in schools, for organizational change and similar matters.
Even so, many educational decisions, whether in the classroom or on
a national scale, will, for a long time yet, have to be taken in the
absence of firm knowledge derived from research. Nor perhaps will

it be possible or desirable to wait for the results of long-term action studies before implementing decisions on a wide scale. Many curricular changes are like this at present and will probably always be so; so may be such decisions as whether to raise the school leaving age. In such cases, however, two forms of research inquiry are valuable— limited feasibility studies to explore and anticipate the snags and likely difficulties of an innovation; and in-built evaluation to check —in time to influence or even radically change development— whether the proposed aims are in fact being realized.

What has been discussed so far represents an immediate intensification of more or less traditional forms of research activity in education; it is in fact the first stage in the transition from the partial examination of partial problems—for which research workers have been so often (and by and large so unjustly) criticized. Many of the most important problems of education are such that the methods and concepts so far described are not the best means of attack. Nor can these problems be even approximately studied by simple applications of methods of any of the basic social sciences, important as their contributions may be. We can only hope to move toward an understanding of the complex central core of the educational process, when resources allow us to develop and maintain considerable multi-disciplinary teams applying themselves to studies of real classrooms over considerable periods of time. We must examine the varieties of teaching task, the tissue of interactions between pupil and teacher, the factors which influence school and classroom climates, and, through them, the motivations of pupils to learn or to resist learning. We must also explore the school as a plastic, transitional community, set between the family and society. If we can carry out a reasonably well-specified job analysis of teaching in its many facets we shall have some certain basis for teacher training—at present little more than an apprenticeship with educational overtones.

Such an increase in the relevance and power of educational research cannot come about simply through the activities of research workers themselves. It involves some fundamental rethinking of the concepts of research by which we work, and of the relation between practice and research activity. Basically it is true to say that, while very many teachers and educationists are aware that there is or should be an educational technology, most regard this as peripheral. On the other hand, many research workers in the social sciences fail to distinguish between particular scientific methods—those hallowed by success in the natural sciences—and scientific method as a way of analyzing experience. They tend to fall victim to the prestige of the natural sciences and strive to prove themselves respectable by approximating as closely as possible to their procedures. Even if one could do so, the attempt (in, say, an experiment in teaching poetry) systematically to isolate and vary one factor after another—social class, cultural background, sex, ability, teacher competence, prior experience, and so forth—would be a failure on two counts: that of defining and separating the factors to be varied; and that—which most teachers know in their bones—of failing to see that in the educational process the whole is qualitatively different from the sum of its parts. The crucial characteristics of good scientific method are an attempt to diminish (and to estimate and allow for) the bias of the observer, with known degrees of error, and a careful objectivity in recording and reporting which allows rigorous comparison with experiments of a similar kind conducted by others.

If we are really to approach such questions as what makes children learn, how they are motivated, what their aspirations are, and how true equality of opportunity may be provided for pupils of differing kinds from differing environments, our laboratory is the school. This implies two other things. The research team itself must have within it practicing teachers; and it must collaborate with teachers actually engaged in the classroom. For practical as well as scientific reasons, it is probably best to base the initial research work on a number of experimental and laboratory schools closely associated with research institutions and constituting the equivalent of the physicists' or chemists' laboratory. Such schools and classes would provide the facilities for the close study of real educational situations, for action research and development work in their initial stages. Once some clear insight or theory is gained, or a new development has shown a reasonable prospect of success in these manifestly favorable circumstances, then should come field trials on a larger scale in a sample of ordinary schools, with adequate evaluation to explore whether generalization to the entire system is possible and under what conditions.[22]

This concept has implications for the role and training of teachers and of educational research workers. There must be a basis of common respect and common experience—all or most of the research workers should have had teacher training and real experience, all or most teachers should have at least a minimum knowledge of research. Just as agricultural research and medical research are heavily tributary to the natural and biological sciences, so educational research will depend upon scientists outside the educational field and will need to employ some in its teams. Just, too, as many of the more important research problems in medicine or agriculture have arisen from the work and experiment of the busy but inquiring doctor or farmer, so we may hope that teachers, part of whose training has turned their attention to the scientific study of education, will identify problems, spearhead their study, and in many cases move over themselves to full-time research. Indeed the great hope of real advance lies in making the present barriers between professional practice and professional research really permeable, so that it becomes normal for a career in teaching to include a period of full-time research.

There will probably always be aspects of education where the teacher's intuition and insight are more valuable as guides than scientific knowledge. Education too is not static; it is in fact highly responsive to changes in society, particularly to changes in the beliefs and values held almost below the threshold of consciousness by parents and teachers or implied by the way the world confronts the young. Because of this, the established facts of one generation of research workers tend to seem to be the fallacies to be attacked by the next. We shall be nearer the truth if we say that advances in knowledge in as changing a field as education will be of the nature of successive approximations rather than securely established platforms from which to launch the next probe. However—even if we regard education as unequivocally an art rather than a science—there is an advancing technology which can subtend even the greatest artist and make his work easier and more effective. Most of us are not great artists in education; and the major value of the technological advance which we can hope for from research is that we can considerably improve, by taking thought, what it is that we do. At least we can define the possible, count and measure the cost of alternatives, challenge superstition with facts, and define the area within which value-loaded choices have to be made. If this is done well, it will increase the central responsibility of the teacher for choosing that which he believes to be *good;* but it will also make it more possible for him to carry out his decision hopefully.

This vision of the future of educational research in the United Kingdom appears to lie somewhere between the modest view outlined earlier in this chapter and the hopes of the National Institute of Education. In the degree and rapidity of change anticipated, it is not far from the view of President Johnson's Educational Task Force of 1964. It is a thoughtful analysis of needs for knowledge by the practitioner and presents a plausible system of activities and institutions to meet these needs.

At the beginning of this chapter the comment was made that the future cannot be predicted with precision and that it will be full of surprises. Even so, it is still possible to make a few general statements about the future. There will always be a need and a demand for increased knowledge about the educational enterprise. The demand may not be great, but it will be sufficient to support some continuing research activities. Civilized societies have learned the value of verified knowledge and the hazards of operating with only tradition as a guide. During the past seventy-five years the need for verified knowledge about education has become widely recognized.

Educational practitioners of tomorrow will seek more verified knowledge than those of today, just as today's practitioners seek more than did their predecessors. Albeit slowly, professionals in a modern industrial society recognize that most of their clients expect results and are not satisfied with the elegance of their rituals alone. Hence, future practitioners will be utilizing relevant knowledge that was not employed by an earlier generation. The uncertain questions are: how rapidly will new knowledge be used and how widely will the uses of new knowledge extend?

We can be sure that there will be "middlemen" in the future. They may not be called by the same names—workshop leaders, action researchers, staff trainers, instructors of in-service programs, developers, authors of textbooks, editors, publishers, salespersons—but they will be there. Both the lay public and practitioners recognize the need for new learning systems to meet new educational problems and the need for new devices to aid teachers.

These general statements are highly probable. But the extent of support, the size of the research and development community, the degree of concentration or decentralization, and the location of the functions among the different institutions are the matters about which the future cannot be predicted with precision.

Notes

1. Kenneth Boulding, "Predictive Reliability and the Future: The Need for Uncertainty," in *The Future of Education: Perspectives on Tomorrow's Schooling,*" ed. Louis Rubin (Rockleigh, N.J.: Allyn and Bacon, 1975), Chap. 3.

2. National Institute of Education Task Force on Resources Planning, *Building*

Capacity for Renewal and Reform (Washington, D.C.: National Institute of Education, 1974).

3. "NIE Plan to Build Educational R & D Capacity," *Educational Researcher* 3 (February 1974): 14-19.

4. U.S. Office of Education, *Educational Research and Development in the United States* (Washington, D.C.: U.S. Government Printing Office, 1970), 174-175.

5. Deborah L. Eaton, "NIE Attacks the Reading and Language Skills Problem," *American Education* 10 (May 1974): 35-36.

6. W. D. Wall, "The Future of Educational Research," *Educational Research* 10 (June 1968): 163-169.

7. It is not suggested that every teacher should or could approach every decision in this elaborate way! If he did, the profession would resemble the self-conscious centipede blocked by a failure to decide which foot to put down first.

8. J. S. MacPherson, *Eleven-year-olds Grow Up* (London: University of London Press, 1958); James Maxwell, *The Level and Trend of National Intelligence* (London: University of London Press, 1961); Scottish Council for Research in Education, *Scottish Scholastic Survey* (London: University of London Press, 1953); *id., Social Implications of the 1947 Scottish Mental Survey* (London: University of London Press, 1953).

9. D. A. Pidgeon, "National Survey of the Ability and Attainment of Children at Three Age Levels," *British Journal of Educational Psychology* 30, Pt. 2 (June 1960): 124-133.

10. Ministry of Education, *Reading Ability* (London: H.M. Stationery Office, 1950); *id., Standards of Reading, 1948-1956*, Pamphlet No. 32 (London: H.M. Stationery Office, 1957).

11. J. E. Floud *et al., Social Class and Educational Opportunity* (London: Heinemann, 1957).

12. J. W. B. Douglas, *The Home and the School* (London: MacGibbon and Kee, 1964).

13. Alfred Yates and D. A. Pidgeon, *Admission to Grammar Schools* (London: Newnes, 1957).

14. *International Study of Achievement in Mathematics: A Comparison of Twelve Countries*, Vols. I and II, ed. Torsten Husén (Stockholm: Almqvist and Wiksell; New York: John Wiley, 1967); D. A. Pidgeon, *Achievement in Mathematics* (Slough: National Foundation for Educational Research, 1967).

15. Douglas, *The Home and the School.*

16. J. M. Morris, *Reading in the Primary School* (London: Newnes, 1959); *id., Standards and Progress in Reading* (Slough: National Foundation for Educational Research, 1966); Margaret Cox, *The Challenge of Reading Failure* (Slough: National Foundation for Educational Research, 1968).

17. E. J. Goodacre, *Reading in Infant Classes* (Slough: National Foundation for Educational Research, 1967); *id., Teachers and Their Pupils' Home Background* (Slough: National Foundation for Educational Research, 1968).

18. Clare Burstall, "The French Project: An Interim Report," *New Research in Education* 1 (June 1967): 76-81.

19. J. B. Biggs, *Mathematics and the Conditions of Learning* (Slough: National Foundation for Educational Research, 1967); J. D. Williams, "Effecting Educational Change: Some Notes on the Reform of Primary School Mathematics Teaching," *Educational Research* 8 (June 1966): 191-195.

20. John A. Downing *et al., The i.t.a. Symposium* (Slough: National Foundation for Educational Research, 1967).

21. N. E. Svensson, *Ability Grouping and Scholastic Achievement* (Stockholm: Almqvist and Wiksell, 1962).

22. As is done in the RFSSR. See Michael Dunlop Young, *Innovation and Research in Education,* appendix by W. D. Wall (London: Routledge and Kegan Paul, 1965).